T5-AWJ-963

Government Controls on Transport
An African Case

Government Controls on Transport

An African Case

Edwin T. Haefele and Eleanor B. Steinberg

The Brookings Institution

TRANSPORT RESEARCH PROGRAM

Washington, D.C.   [1965]

THE BROOKINGS INSTITUTION is an independent organization devoted to nonpartisan research, education, and publication in economics, government, foreign policy, and the social sciences generally. Its principal purposes are to aid in the development of sound public policies and to promote public understanding of issues of national importance.

The Institution was founded December 8, 1927, to merge the activities of the Institute for Government Research, founded in 1916, the Institute of Economics, founded in 1922, and the Robert Brookings Graduate School of Economics and Government, founded in 1924.

The general administration of the Institution is the responsibility of a self-perpetuating Board of Trustees. The trustees are likewise charged with maintaining the independence of the staff and fostering the most favorable conditions for creative research and education. The immediate direction of the policies, program, and staff of the Institution is vested in the President, assisted by the division directors and an advisory council, chosen from the professional staff of the Institution.

In publishing a study, the Institution presents it as a competent treatment of a subject worthy of public consideration. The interpretations and conclusions in such publications are those of the author or authors and do not purport to represent the views of the other staff members, officers, or trustees of the Brookings Institution.

Foreword

ONE OF THE IMPORTANT factors in determining the need for new transport investment in the emerging nations is the degree of utilization of existing facilities. Utilization is in turn affected by the kinds of governmental restrictions on use which may be imposed for economic or political reasons. Where existing facilities are shared by more than one nation, as they are in much of Africa, governmental controls on transport become more complicated. They become subject to international politics as well as to national economics.

The present study was undertaken to illustrate this situation and to call attention to the effect such problems can have on definitions of investment needs. It is the third publication of the Brookings Transport Research Program, financed by a grant from the Agency for International Development.

The reading committee included A. Robert Sadove, The World Bank; George W. Wilson, Indiana University; and Andrew F. Westwood of the Brookings staff. Jane Lecht edited the manuscript. The Transport Research Program, under the direction of Wilfred Owen, is conducted in the Economic Studies Division, headed by Joseph A. Pechman.

The authors wish to acknowledge with special thanks the help of the following people: S. G. Watts, Benguela Railway Company; R. F. Norman, Leopold Walford Shipping, Ltd.; R. Wautelet, Ancienne Compagnie du Chemin de Fer du Bas-Congo au Katanga; Taylor Ostrander and Erasmus H. Kloman, Jr., American Metals Climax; John Lascelles, D. K. Cattell and B. D. Napper, Roan Selection Trust; Gordon Goundrey, Ministry of

Finance, Government of Zambia; Marshall Clark, Anglo-American, Ltd.; F. Sander, The World Bank; Peter F. Barrett, formerly Counsellor, Minister for Rhodesia and Nyasaland Affairs, British Embassy in Washington; and Delbert O. Gordon, U.S. Department of Commerce. Brookings colleagues who were especially helpful included Wilfred Owen, Robert T. Brown, Samuel Weiner, Nuhad J. Kanaan, Virginia C. Whitney, Marian S. Magg, and Edna Lusher.

Opinions expressed by the authors do not purport to represent the views of the persons listed above, the Agency for International Development, or the trustees, officers, or other staff members of the Brookings Institution.

Robert D. Calkins
President

September 1965
Washington, D.C.

Contents

Appendixes

Index

Figures

Tables

Introduction

THIS STUDY EXAMINES the institutions, policies, and controls which determine certain transport patterns in a region of the underdeveloped world—South Central Africa, an area more than two-thirds the size of the United States.

Within this region are both newly independent nations and countries still held by colonial powers. Despite the fact that some of these nations are "new" and all have limited transport facilities, they are not free of transport controls. All share a colonial background from which they inherited a transport system with institutional arrangements nearly as complex as those of the mother countries. Furthermore, most of the government controls on transport were established in response to narrow or short-term problems with little regard for the long-run needs of an economy or its future development.

The objective of this study is to suggest means of forestalling unneeded transport investments and of preventing the continuation of uneconomic uses of existing facilities. The focus is on rail transport which is of overriding importance in the area and on copper which is the most important single source of traffic and revenues as well as a key factor in a series of agreements and controls to assure certain traffic to particular rail routes. The emphasis is on traffic which crosses national boundaries. It was the divergence of national interests from regional economic interests that established the patterns for controls on transport which have emerged.

These controls, combined with present political alignments, are compelling some African governments to consider an expensive new rail link from Zambia to the Indian Ocean—an investment

1

FIGURE 1. *Railroads Serving Central Africa*

which cannot be justified on economic grounds. An alternative to this investment is revision of existing treaties and agreements on traffic and rates to increase utilization of the existing rail facilities.

The existing rail network consists of the main rail lines of Angola, the Republic of the Congo (formerly the Belgian Congo), Zambia (Northern Rhodesia until October 1964), Rhodesia (formerly Southern Rhodesia), and Mozambique. The Central Line of Tanganyika, while not connected to the rest of the system except by lake transshipment, must be considered in any economic treatment of the area. The railways in Angola and the Congo are still essentially privately owned while the other railways are government owned. The area of the region served by this rail system is roughly 1,700 miles (East-West) by 1,400 miles (North-South) or 2,380,000 square miles. (See Figure 1 for a map identifying the principal rail lines.)

Three countries in the region—the Congo, Zambia, and Tanganyika—are newly independent, while Angola and Mozambique are firmly under Portuguese control. Rhodesia, while technically under British suzerainty, manages its own affairs through a white minority government. Larger political issues already intrude upon railway policy and may be expected to do so even more in the near future.

The Importance of Copper

In discussing rail transport patterns and the institutional arrangements determining these patterns in South Central Africa, we have selected the case of copper because it highlights the interplay among private companies, railways, and governments which determines policy; because the copper mines are located roughly in the center of this region; and because copper is hauled on all the railways in question. In terms of value, copper is the leading export of both the Congo and Zambia.[1] In the years im-

[1] In recent years, manganese has surpassed copper in the Congo as the leading product and export in terms of tonnage. However, manganese is exported as an ore, whereas copper is refined before shipment abroad. The value of manganese exports relative to copper exports is quite low.

mediately prior to Congolese independence in 1960, copper accounted for roughly one-third of the Congo's total exports in terms of value. The significance of copper to Zambia is even greater. In recent years copper exports have earned more than nine-tenths of the country's export revenues. Furthermore, since the opening of the first railway in this part of Africa, the movement of copper has been the subject of numerous transport agreements as well as the object of much controversy.

Copper earnings are important not only to the exporting countries, but also to the railways which carry copper to the ocean ports. Three of the railways receive a significant proportion of their freight revenues from this traffic. In the accounting year ending June 30, 1963, copper traffic accounted for 27.6 percent of the total freight revenues of the Rhodesia Railways. During the calendar year 1963 copper revenues (based on a conservative estimate[2] of £8 revenue per ton of copper carried) accounted for 18 percent of the total revenues of the Benguela Railway.

Revenue details are not available for railways in the Congo. However, the fact that in 1959 copper accounted for 27.3 percent of the total export tonnage moving along the national route from Elisabethville to Port Francqui destined for shipment from Matadi indicates the importance of copper traffic to the Compagnie du Chemin de Fer du Bas-Congo au Katanga (BCK).

Present Railway Routes

A comparison of the basic characteristics of the existing railways into Central Africa is presented in Table 1. Data from 1960 are used in order to present the position of the Congolese railways prior to their disruption after independence. The table indicates (1) that, on all railroads except the CFL, copper is hauled

[2] The freight rate on copper from the Congo via the Benguela is a private, negotiated rate, the proceeds of which are shared with the Compagnie du Chemin de Fer du Bas-Congo au Katanga (BCK) which is the originating line. The £8 estimate is based on the published Benguela rate for copper from Zambia. The Congo rate is acknowledged to be at least as high and to be based on the price of copper in the world market.

TABLE 1. *Railways in Central Africa, Basic Data, 1960*[a]
(Tonnage in metric tons)

Railway	Country	Total Route Mileage	Route Miles Over Which Copper is Hauled	Gauge	Freight Tonnage Carried	Copper Tonnage Carried
BCK	Congo	1,588	1,500	3'6"	4,396,000	352,265
CFL	Congo	596	169	3'6"	377,300	2,030
Benguela Railway	Angola	879	838	3'6"	1,822,555	177,142
Rhodesia Railways	Zambia and Rhodesia	2,599	1,518	3'6"	10,215,077[b]	821,799
EAR&H[c]	Tanganyika	1,283[d]	780	3'3⅜"	617,763	2,030

Sources: Figures for route mileage and for number of route miles over which copper is hauled are from documents of the CFL and BCK; 1960 and 1961 Annual Reports of Rhodesia Railways, Benguela Railway, and East African Railways and Harbours; and *World Railways, 1961–62*, Sampson Low's, Ltd. (London, 1962). Freight tonnage figures are from *Bulletin Mensuel*, Comité des Transporteurs au Congo (Brussels, January 1963) for CFL and BCK; 1960 and 1961 Annual Reports of Rhodesia Railways, Benguela Railway, and EAR&H. Copper tonnage figures are from same sources as freight except for CFL figure, which is based on EAR&H data, and Benguela figure, supplied by London Office, Benguela Railway Company.

[a] Mileage figures and figures for freight and copper tonnage are for 1960. This year was used because it was the last year during which Congolese railways were operating normally. Figures for Rhodesia Railways are for fiscal year ending June 30, 1960.

[b] Figure for all sections of Rhodesia Railways north and east of Bulawayo (i.e., section in Bechuanaland is excluded).

[c] Central Tanganyika Line only.

[d] Figure includes Central Line plus branches.

over a high proportion of the total mileage of the railway, and (2) that the amount of copper *tonnage* compared to total freight *tonnage* is quite small in all cases.

The four existing routes for copper, as shown in Figure 2, are as follows:

Route No. 1: All rail via BCK and/or Rhodesia Railways-Mozambique Railways from Katanga and Zambia to the ports of Beira and Lourenço Marques in Mozambique.

Route No. 2: All rail via Rhodesia Railways and/or BCK-Benguela Railway from Zambia and Katanga to the port of Lobito in Angola.

Route No. 3: Rail-river-rail route via BCK-Kasai River-Chemin de Fer Matadi-Leopoldville from Katanga to the port of Matadi in the Congo.

Route No. 4: Rail-lake-rail route via BCK-Compagnie des Chemins de Fer du Congo Supérieur aux Grands Lacs Africains

FIGURE 2. *Major Copper Export Routes*

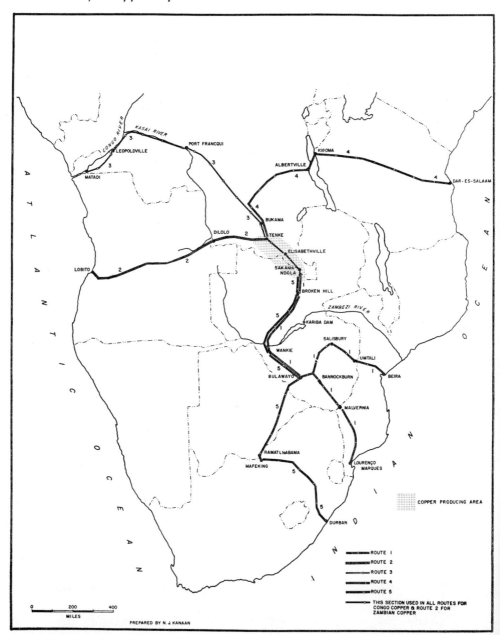

COPPER PRODUCING AREA

ROUTE 1
ROUTE 2
ROUTE 3
ROUTE 4
ROUTE 5
THIS SECTION USED IN ALL ROUTES FOR
CONGO COPPER & ROUTE 2 FOR
ZAMBIAN COPPER

0   200   400
MILES

PREPARED BY N. J. KANAAN

6

TABLE 2. *Shipment of Copper from the Congo and Zambia via Principal Export Routes, 1953–63*[a]
(In metric tons)

	1953	1954	1955	1956	1957	1958	1959	1960	1961	1962	1963
Beira and Lourenço Marques[b]											
Congo	59,457	76,726	68,746	76,273	71,982	69,330	81,750	117,199	113,263	68,390	81,377
Zambia	346,146	373,991	345,601	354,206	371,877	317,138	447,567	493,914	532,192	525,684	552,124
Total	405,603	450,717	414,347	430,479	443,859	386,468	529,317	611,113	645,455	594,074	633,501
Lobito[c]											
Congo	34,188	42,026	44,209	47,555	47,443	48,165	56,163	114,007	178,175	219,257	153,089
Zambia	0	0	0	0	31,139	47,219	81,879	63,135	20,730	195	5
Total	34,188	42,026	44,209	47,555	78,582	95,384	138,042	177,142	198,905	219,452	153,094
Matadi[d]											
Congo	101,974	96,281	90,251	100,504	83,833	84,336	103,830	57,736	0	70	12,509
Zambia	0	0	0	0	0	0	0	0	0	0	0
Total	101,974	96,281	90,251	100,504	83,833	84,336	103,830	57,736	0	70	12,509

[a] Port authority sources are used for some of these statistics; railway figures are used for others. Figures from these two different sources are not precisely comparable. All copper hauled on a railway to a port does not necessarily move out of the port that same year. This is due to the fact that some is warehoused and also that shipments leaving the mines or refineries at the end of a calendar year often do not leave the port until the beginning of the following year. Use of both port and rail figures was necessary because all-port or all-rail figures were not available. Figures do not include copper shipped to the Republic of South Africa.

[b] Source: *Comércio Externo*, Província de Moçambique, Direcção dos Serviços e Estatística Geral, 1953–56; 1957–63, Roan Selection Trust, Ltd. (Salisbury and Lusaka offices).

[c] Source: London Office, Benguela Railway Company, Ltd.

[d] Source: *La Situation Économique du Congo Belge et du Ruanda-Urundi*, Direction des Études Économiques, Brussels, 1953–59. For years 1960–63, Union Minière du Haut-Katanga, correspondence dated March 3, 1965.

7

TABLE 3. *Annual Smelter Production of Copper in the Congo and Zambia, 1953–63*[a]
(In metric tons)

Year	Congo	Zambia	Year	Congo	Zambia
1953	214,150	368,400	1959	282,097	539,866
1954	220,833	384,691	1960	302,254	567,851
1955	235,109	348,686	1961	295,203	568,941
1956	249,966	389,643	1962	295,239	547,748
1957	242,246	422,895	1963	269,927	576,019
1958	237,734	380,970			

Source: U.S. Department of the Interior, *Minerals Yearbook*, Vol. I, 1958 and 1963.

[a] Discrepancies between production and export figures may be attributed to (1) small shipments through other exits, such as Pointe Noire and Republic of South Africa ports, (2) warehousing, (3) differences among sources as to what is included under "copper export."

(CFL)-Lake Tanganyika-East African Railways from Katanga and Zambia to the port of Dar es Salaam in Tanganyika.[3]

A fifth possible route, now seldom used for copper export, is the old South African route, for which a line was built from Mafeking to Bulawayo in Southern Rhodesia. Mafeking was connected with the port of Durban by a rail line which was and is part of the South African rail system. (See Figure 2.) While Zambia no longer uses Durban for the export of copper, copper from Zambia and the Congo destined for use in South Africa has utilized this rail route in recent years.

The recent history of copper exports via these routes is detailed in Table 2, and copper production figures are found in Table 3.

[3] Detailed geographic analyses of these rail transport routes and their ports have been made by William Hance and Irene S. van Dongen in a series of articles based on research done for the Office of Naval Research of the United States Government. One of the implicit conclusions of these articles was that irrational port and rail investments and poor routing decisions were being made in South Central Africa. The articles include:

"Beira, Mozambique Gateway to Central Africa," *Annals of the Association of American Geographers*, Vol. 47 (December 1957).

"Dar es Salaam, the Port and its Tributary Area," *Annals of the Association of American Geographers*, Vol. 48 (December 1958).

"Lourenço Marques in Delagoa Bay," *Economic Geography* (July 1957).

"Matadi, Focus of Belgian African Transport," *Annals of the Association of American Geographers*, Vol. 48 (March 1958).

"The Port of Lobito and the Benguela Railway," *The Geographical Review* (American Geographical Society), Vol. 46, No. 4, 1956.

Table 2 shows a more than fourfold increase from 1953 through 1963 in the use of Lobito for copper shipments and approximately a 41 percent increase in the use of Mozambique ports of Beira and Lourenço Marques for copper export over the same period. The figures for Matadi reflect modest fluctuations from one year to the next, until 1960, when the decline was marked. Almost total discontinuation of the use of Matadi for copper exports in 1961 and 1962 reflects not a decline in Congolese copper production (which Table 3 figures indicate was maintained surprisingly well) but, rather, an almost complete breakdown in the Congo transport system due to the post-independence hostilities.

The pattern of distribution, shown in Table 2, is the result of the history of rail development in Africa and agreements among colonial governments and commercial enterprises. An understanding of how this pattern was set is essential to the analysis of present problems.

CHAPTER I

Background of Transport Patterns in South Central Africa

AN HISTORICAL SKETCH of early railway develop-
ment in South Central Africa is a prerequisite for an understanding of the allocation of traffic among the railways in this region in
recent years.

The division of traffic among the various railways has been and
is determined to a large extent by agreements among private
companies and railways, by railway tariff policies, and by ocean
shipping rates. Other factors include political relations among the
colonial powers or among the countries themselves, the chrono-
logical order in which the railways were opened, and the allocation of the original mining and railway concessions.

The origins of many of these factors go back to the late nineteenth and early twentieth centuries when the interior of Africa
was being opened up by the construction of railways. Although
the nineteenth century is often regarded today as an era when
private risk capital was readily available for investment in much
of what is now referred to as the underdeveloped world, this is a
somewhat nostalgic and not altogether accurate view. In most in-
stances, the colonial power or its agent, by either choice or necessity, became very much involved in the building of the railways. Not only did the state grant railway concessions, but in the
cases of Tanganyika and the Congo, the colonial governments actually participated directly in the financing of the railways. Furthermore, in the mineral-rich colonies of the interior—the Congo
and the Rhodesias—the rail concessions and the mineral conces-

10

sions were granted to the same financial interests as an inducement to the mutual development of both mining and transport.

In the Belgian Congo and the Rhodesias, the principal motivation behind the willingness of the colonial authorities to assume the initiative in railway development was a desire to consolidate their position in the colonies. King Leopold of Belgium was determined to build a national rail system extending from Katanga Province north to the western and eastern parts of the Congo, while one of the primary goals of Cecil Rhodes' life was to build a "Cape-to-Cairo" railway running entirely through British possessions. The major inducement for building railways from the standpoint of private financial interests and the colonial powers in possession of the coasts of this part of Africa was the mineral wealth of the Congo and Northern Rhodesia. The colonial governments of Tanganyika and of Mozambique and Angola, as well as the railway concessionaires, hoped to make money by transporting minerals from the interior to the sea.

In the following brief account of the development of the major railways in Central Africa, particular attention is given to the factors which assured certain traffic to various railways, as well as to the methods used by the railways or the governments to capture traffic.

Rhodesia Railways

In the 1890's, two railways were being built more or less simultaneously to link the landlocked Rhodesias with the coast. A line was being constructed from Beira on the Mozambique coast to Salisbury in Southern Rhodesia to provide means of transport and communications for the settlers in and around Salisbury. Another line was being built from Mafeking in South Africa through Bechuanaland to Bulawayo in Southern Rhodesia. (See Figure 2.) Further extensions northward enabled the railway to reach Broken Hill in Northern Rhodesia in 1906. In the mind of Cecil Rhodes, this railway was to constitute part of a "Cape-to-Cairo" railway, and this in itself was sufficient justification to build it.

The mineral wealth of Broken Hill was presented as an economic justification to investors for what was essentially a romantic venture. However, the Northern Rhodesian mineral resources were not developed to any significant extent until the early 1930's; in the meantime, the railway was greatly underutilized.

The haphazard state of planning with regard to potential traffic and the spirit of adventure on the part of the railway builders is reflected in the following account by an engineer who had worked on the project:

> After the rush came the reaction, when, as I have mentioned, the goal we had been racing after at top speed failed to come up to expectations, and there was nothing like the traffic that had been promised. The necessity of obtaining additional traffic to make the long extension pay was naturally apparent, and it became imperative to carry the line still farther north to tap the extensive mineral deposits of Katanga. . . . On our return to the railhead at Broken Hill, after an absence of six weeks, the terminus looked very forlorn and deserted. . . . The Cape-to-Cairo Railway came to an end in the middle of a burnt-out vlei [marsh] without even a buffer-stop at the rail terminus. Beside it stood a solitary telegraph post, and in this atmosphere of desolation it languished for several years.[1]

The British South Africa Company, often referred to as the "Chartered," or BSA, was the governing authority in the Rhodesias and thus held all of the mineral rights and also monopolized railway transportation. Even after the British government took over the administration of the Rhodesias in 1924, BSA retained the mineral rights and owned all of the railways.

BSA-owned railways had little difficulty maintaining a monopoly with regard to the transport of Rhodesian minerals, even after the arrival on the scene in 1931 of the Benguela Railway, a potential competitor for the traffic. (Route 2 in Figure 2.) The ability of BSA to stave off for many years the thrust of competition for Rhodesian traffic presented by the Benguela-Lobito route goes back to the legal arrangements drawn up in connection with the financing, construction, and operation of the Rhodesia-Katanga Junction Railway. As indicated in the quotation from H. F. Varian cited earlier, BSA in the early 1900's felt compelled to extend

[1] H. F. Varian, *Some African Milestones* (Worcester and London: Trinity Press, 1935), pp. 127-29.

their railway northward from Broken Hill in order to attract Katanga mineral traffic (inasmuch as the mineral wealth of Northern Rhodesia was not yet being exploited). At the same time, Sir Robert Williams, founder of Tanganyika Concessions Limited (TCL)—which later financed the construction of the Benguela Railway and is today principal shareholder of the Benguela Railway Company—was seeking an export route for Katanga minerals.

In an agreement between BSA and TCL, the former granted TCL certain mineral rights and the right to build a railway from Broken Hill to the Congo border as well as branch lines to various mines. In return for these concessions, TCL undertook to raise the capital necessary to build the railway. Under the agreement, BSA retained the right to purchase the line and branches in 1918, or at the end of every subsequent five-year period, on six months' notice. In 1928 BSA served notice of its intention to purchase the Rhodesia-Katanga Junction Railway, and the final transfer of ownership took place in 1929.

All Rhodesian mineral traffic must move on this rail line between Broken Hill and Sakania in order to go either to Angolan or Mozambique ports. (See Figure 2.) It is apparent, in retrospect, that BSA's right to purchase this 132-mile rail link was a key factor in determining routes for Northern Rhodesian copper. Had TCL continued as owner of the Rhodesia-Katanga Junction Railway, the bargaining power of TCL on behalf of the Benguela Railway as a transporter of Rhodesian minerals would have been substantially strengthened.

Although the Benguela Railway in its early years did not carry any Rhodesian minerals, a formal agreement was concluded in the depression year 1936 between Rhodesia Railways and the Northern Rhodesian copper companies. The agreement provided that the copper companies would ship all of their copper on Rhodesia Railways for the next 20 years in exchange for fixed rates (around £3 per ton) on the copper as well as even lower fixed rates on coal from the Wankie Colliery in Southern Rhodesia, which was used by the copper mines for power and for ore processing. In addition, to assure a two-way traffic—coal to the copper mines and copper from mine to port—the copper companies agreed not to develop hydroelectric power.

Rhodesia Railways, in addition to assuring itself of all Rhodesian copper traffic by means of agreements guaranteeing low rates, also attracted agricultural traffic by offering exceptionally low rates on commodity exports and farm imports. The purpose was to assist in agricultural development, thereby building a base for increasing agricultural traffic in the future. In order to compensate for these low rates, high rates, relative to Rhodesian copper rates, were charged on Katanga (Congo) copper. These rates were possible because the Katanga copper mines were also very much dependent upon Wankie coal from Southern Rhodesia. Because of that dependence the rates persisted at a high level even after the opening of the Benguela Railway line.

Toward the end of 1956, when the 1936 agreement between the copper companies and Rhodesia Railways[2] was about to expire, Rhodesia Railways was forced to negotiate an agreement allowing a small amount of Northern Rhodesian copper to be exported via the Benguela route. This agreement resulted from intensive pressure by the copper producers who wanted to use the route through Angola because of long delays on the Rhodesia Railways-Beira route, caused by post-World War II traffic congestion. In 1957 Rhodesia Railways, the Benguela Railway, and the Compagnie du Chemin de Fer du Bas-Congo au Katanga (BCK) entered into a four-year "Tripartite Agreement"[3] under which rail rates on Northern Rhodesian copper were equalized from all copper stations to the ports of Lobito, Beira, and Lourenço Marques. The through rate on copper for the three ports was established at £14.17.0. The amount of copper permitted to be shipped out via the BCK-Benguela route during a given year was 10 percent of the railings by the Northern Rhodesian Copper Mines to Beira and Lourenço Marques at the time the Agreement was entered into, plus 50 percent of any additional tonnage available for export via the Mozambique ports, subject

[2] In 1949 the Rhodesia Railways system was nationalized and assigned to a statutory authority composed of the Prime Minister of Southern Rhodesia, the Minister of Mines and Transport, the Governor of Northern Rhodesia, and the High Commissioner of Bechuanaland, Basutoland, and Swaziland. Responsibility for the system was transferred four years later to the Government of the Federation of Rhodesia and Nyasaland, formed by the British government in 1953 and dissolved at the end of 1963.

[3] See Appendix A for text.

to a maximum of 20 percent of the total tonnage available for export.

By the time the Agreement was renewed in July 1960, Rhodesia Railways had expanded their capacity by extensive improvements and additions in rolling stock. Immediately after the renewal of the Agreement, a special discount rate of £9.10.6, unilaterally instituted by Rhodesia Railways, went into effect on the amount of copper permitted under the terms of the Tripartite Agreement to be shipped out via the Benguela-Lobito route.[4]

Although the BCK and the Benguela protested the discount rate, they did not choose to match it. The impetus for the establishment of the discount rate was provided by the Federal Government of Rhodesia and Nyasaland. Historically, the Federal Government had a stronger attachment to the exclusive use of Rhodesia Railways system than did Northern Rhodesia, which traditionally wanted to be able to utilize the Benguela route as well as Rhodesia Railways.

At the same time that the discount rate was announced, Rhodesia Railways informed the other parties to the Agreement that a maximum of 36,000 tons of copper a year would be permitted to move out via Lobito. These unilateral actions on the part of Rhodesia Railways were never actually written into the renewal agreement. Since the latter half of 1960, almost all Northern Rhodesian copper has moved out on Rhodesia Railways. Because of the attractiveness of the discount rate, the copper companies have not utilized even the 36,000 ton quota. (See Table 2.)

Congo Railways

At the turn of the century two important factors helped stimulate railway development in the Belgian Congo. One was the desire of King Leopold to construct a national route diagonally through the middle of the Congo. The second was the need for an

---

[4] As a result of a 10 percent rate increase on all goods traffic instituted by Rhodesia Railways in September 1962, the discount rate was raised to £10.9.7, and the regular through rate on copper to the Angolan and Mozambique ports became £16.6.8.

alternate route for shipping Katanga minerals from mine to port. Because of the great distance involved in the proposed national route (or *any* all-Congo route), an economic alternative for the export of Katanga minerals meant, inevitably, the use of a rail line running partly through the Congo but primarily through adjacent colonies owned by foreign (non-Belgian) powers.

For this reason, almost from the moment of its conception, the Congo national route was a controversial issue. The ocean terminal for the route was to be the man-made port of Matadi, situated 80 miles up the Congo River from the Atlantic Ocean on the only scrap of land owned by the Belgians with an outlet to the sea. This land was exceptionally unpromising for the construction of a port; the terrain through which the route itself was to be constructed was equally unpromising. In addition, the distance of the national route would be much greater for shipments to and from Katanga, for example, than would be the distance between Katanga and Lobito or between Katanga and Beira.[5]

Consequently, a number of practical-minded men were opposed to the proposed national route from the start. Sir Robert Williams, engineer and chairman of Tanganyika Concessions Limited, which obtained a large mineral prospecting concession in Katanga in 1901, referred to the proposed route as "the political railway of His Majesty."[6] Despite this and similar objections, the national route was constructed. It reached Port Francqui, the present transshipment point to the Kasai River, in 1928. In the early 1930's, when the world was in the depths of a depression, the Belgians established a policy of *tout pour la voie nationale.* Every effort, by means of persuasion, rate policy, and other devices, was made to attract as much traffic as possible to the national route.

In 1932 two special tariff systems were introduced, the purpose of which was to induce traffic to flow through Matadi. Both of these rate systems are still in effect today. The essence of the

[5] The original national route, which was a combination river and rail route, was 2,235 miles long and involved seven transshipments. The opening of the Port Francqui-Bukama rail line in 1928 reduced the length to 1,714 miles and the number of transshipments to two. The rail distance between Elisabethville and Lobito is 1,309 miles; between Elisabethville and Beira it is 1,619 miles.

[6] *Union Minière du Haut Katanga 1906-1956* (Brussels: Editions L. Cuypers, 1956), p. 66.

échelles mobiles or "sliding scale" system, which applies to agri-cultural commodities for export, is that rates fluctuate with world commodity prices. A system called *tarifs inter-réseaux,* or "in-terregional tariffs," was established primarily for imports. The purpose of the interregional tariffs was to assure that rates on im-ports coming into the Congo via Matadi were at parity with rates on goods via the shorter and less costly foreign routes (from Lobi-to, Beira, and Dar es Salaam). In 1957, when the interregional tariffs were revised, the ceiling rates on goods imported from Lo-bito to Elisabethville were actually higher than the ceiling rates for goods imported to the same destination from Matadi.[7]

A measure of the success of these tariff systems is shown by the fact that, from the end of World War II to 1960, the year of inde-pendence for the Congo, more than 60 percent of the total annual tonnage of Congolese imports came in via Matadi and its subsidi-ary port, Ango-Ango; the comparable figure for exports was usu-ally between 40 and 50 percent. Were it not for the power of the great mining companies such as Union Minière du Haut Katanga, the export percentage going through Matadi would have been even larger.

The origins of this resistance to the national route date back to the verification of the existence of extensive, rich copper deposits in Katanga by Sir Robert Williams in 1899. Subsequently, Wil-liams' company, Tanganyika Concessions Limited, was granted large mineral prospecting concessions by King Leopold. Williams insisted that the copper must have an economic route to the sea. Thus his first step was to connect the Katanga mines with the Rhodesia Railways, as this required less construction and there-fore less capital than any alternative possibility. Tanganyika Concessions subscribed 40 percent of the capital for the Compag-nie du Chemin de Fer du Katanga. This company built a line from Elisabethville to Sakania at the Congo-Northern Rhodesian borders which connected with the Rhodesia-Katanga Junction Railway, also financed by Tanganyika Concessions. The route from Elisabethville to Ndola was completed by 1910, and Katanga copper began to move on Rhodesia Railways to Beira.

[7] *Bulletin Mensuel,* Comité des Transporteurs au Congo Belge (Brussels, Au-gust 1957), pp. 7-20.

However, Williams' preferred exit for the copper was an old trade route through Angola, the terminal of which was a natural harbor at Lobito Bay. Williams preferred this route not only because it offered the shortest distance from the Katanga mines to a seaport but also because it was on the Atlantic Ocean and therefore as much as 2,500 miles closer to the European markets than the Mozambique ports. In 1902, he secured on behalf of Tanganyika Concessions Limited a concession from the Portuguese government to build a railway along the old trade route. The undertaking was a long and arduous one; the Benguela Railway was not completed until 1931. The Belgians, with their preoccupation with the national route, were not eager to see the completion of this potential competitor. It was only their need for more land (which was owned by Portugal) to expand the port at Matadi that forced the Belgians to agree to build a railway from Tenke in Katanga to connect with the Benguela Railway at the Angolan border. In 1927, the Belgians, in exchange for a small bit of land near Matadi, gave Portugal a small portion of Katanga and agreed to build their part of the railway.

Because of the dependence of the Katanga copper mines on coal from the Wankie Colliery in Southern Rhodesia, approximately 30 percent of Katanga's annual copper exports was shipped out on the Rhodesia Railways to Beira or Lourenço Marques. Then, one-third of Katanga copper (which amounted to roughly 20 percent of total Katanga copper exports) was earmarked for Lobito. This was probably due to the dual role of Tanganyika Concessions as owner of the Benguela Railway and important stockholder in Union Minière du Haut Katanga, owner of virtually all Congo copper mines. The remainder of the copper (usually about 50 percent of the total) went out through Matadi.

Thus, while roughly 50 percent of Congolese copper was exported via the shorter and more economic Benguela Railway and Rhodesia Railways prior to 1960, it should be emphasized that this was made possible not by a deliberate policy of competition, but by other factors which forced the Belgian colonial governments to give way on their policy of *tout pour la voie nationale*. During the period 1961-63, when there was much physical destruction of the Congolese transport system, the national route was used very little, and virtually all copper shipments moved out via the Benguela and Rhodesia Railways. (See Table 2.) Provisional figures for 1964 indicate that the national route is again attracting a sizable share of the copper traffic.

In addition to the diversion of a sizable percentage of copper from the national route, a large percentage of other minerals exported from Katanga, including cobalt, manganese, and zinc, were (and still are) shipped via the Benguela route. For the most part, these raw minerals are mined near the Tenke-Dilolo route (see Figure 2) which connects with the Benguela Railway and could not economically be shipped via Matadi.

Angola and Mozambique Railways

Neither the private financial resources of Lisbon nor the resources of the Portuguese government exchequer were great enough to develop Portugal's colonial railway systems. Consequently, the Portuguese government was forced to grant concessions to foreign companies to build and finance railways in Angola and Mozambique.

An Anglo-Portuguese Convention of 1891 had provided for the construction of a railway from Beira in order to assure the Rhodesias an outlet to the sea. Although Portugal hoped to prevent the British South Africa Company from gaining control of rail and port development in Mozambique, the original concession changed hands and was purchased by BSA interests in 1892. From 1892 to 1949, when the Beira-Umtali line was nationalized, the development of the principal Mozambique railways and the port at Beira was in the hands of the British South Africa Company. Since the opening of the Beira-Umtali line in 1899, a primary function of the Mozambique railways has been to provide an access to the sea for the Rhodesias and Nyasaland. Mozambique, a country with modest known potential for development, receives nearly half of its governmental revenues from transit traffic using its railways and ports.[8]

In addition to transit traffic from the Rhodesias and Nyasaland, Mozambique has long received considerable traffic from South

[8] *Africa Report,* November 1963, p. 31.

Africa. Before the Boer War, the Afrikaaners, who controlled the Transvaal Republic, did not wish to depend on the British-controlled ports of the Cape. Consequently, much of the Transvaal traffic flowed through Lourenço Marques. After the war, Portugal retained its hold on Transvaal traffic by means of an agreement which enabled the Transvaal to recruit native labor in Mozambique in exchange for a promise of 50 percent of the Transvaal's sea-borne traffic. Originally signed in 1909, this agreement, with various amendments pertaining to the percentage of traffic guaranteed Lourenço Marques, and to the treatment of recruited native labor, is still in effect today.[9] Furthermore, in 1950 the governments of Portugal and the United Kingdom concluded a treaty on Beira, which is also in effect today.[10] The principal purpose of this treaty has been to keep Beira operating at full capacity, so that Portugal can finance necessary port improvements required by all users.

In 1955 Lourenço Marques was linked to the copper mines of the Copperbelt and the Congo by the construction of a line from the port to Malvernia, on the Mozambique-Rhodesian border, and from Malvernia to Bannockburn, where it joined the existing Rhodesia Railways system. (See Figure 2.) The impetus for this rail construction was the postwar congestion on the feeder rail lines to Beira and at Beira itself. (It will be recalled that this congestion was also primarily responsible for the Tripartite Agreement of 1957, which permitted Northern Rhodesian copper to move out via the Benguela route.)

With regard to Angola, the Benguela Railway is the only railway in the country which carries transit traffic. The story of the struggle of this railway to capture mineral traffic from the interior of Africa has been told in the sections dealing with the Congo railways and the Rhodesia Railways. Suffice it to add here that the Benguela Railway has always been underutilized in terms of its capacity largely because of the "national route" policies of the Belgian Congo and the Rhodesias.

[9] Great Britain Foreign Office, *British and Foreign State Papers, 1908-09*, Vol. CII, "Convention between the Governments of the Transvaal and the Portuguese Province of Mozambique relating to Natives, Railways and Port, and Commerce and Customs" (London: H.M.S.O., 1913), pp. 110-20.

[10] See Appendix B for text.

Tanganyika Central Railway

The Tanganyika Central Line was built by the German government before World War I, when Tanganyika was a German colony. The hope of carrying mineral traffic from the Congo was a major incentive for the construction of this railway.

The line was begun at Dar es Salaam and reached Kigoma on Lake Tanganyika in 1914. After the war, when Tanganyika became a British mandate under the League of Nations, an Anglo-Belgian agreement permitted Belgium to build its own port facilities at Dar es Salaam and at Kigoma as a means of encouraging Belgian use of Tanganyika's railway and ocean port. The Tanganyika Central Line began to carry an increasing amount of Katanga minerals, and by 1931, almost half of the traffic moving along the line consisted of Katanga copper.

The opening of the Benguela Railway in 1931 and the reorganization of Belgian Congo transport on the basis of a *voie nationale* policy in the 1930's greatly reduced the position of the railway as a significant carrier of Katanga minerals. Since that time, the transit traffic carried by the line has consisted almost entirely of exported agricultural products from the eastern part of the Congo, and from Rwanda and Burundi (formerly the Belgian trustee territory, Ruanda-Urundi), with some imported oil and machinery coming into the Congo via this route. The necessity of transshipment across Lake Tanganyika continues to restrict the growth of transit traffic.

Summary

The hope of capturing mineral traffic was a major incentive for constructing the main rail lines into South Central Africa. Mineral haulage was the sole purpose for the building of the Benguela Railway, which Sir Robert Williams envisioned as a preferred exit for the Katanga copper deposits in which his company, Tanganyika Concessions Limited, held an interest.

In the Rhodesias and in the Belgian Congo the colonial governments exerted their energies toward persuading, inducing, or directing the mining companies located in their colonies to use the national route. This policy was very successful in Northern Rhodesia, where, until 1924, the British South Africa Company (BSA) actually held the colonial governing authority.

Belgian national route policy in the Congo was less successful. Before independence of the Congo in 1960, copper traffic was divided as follows: 30 percent was earmarked for Beira; then two-thirds of the remainder went to Matadi and one-third to Lobito.

The diversion of traffic to Beira resulted from the dependence of the copper mines on coal from the Wankie Colliery in Southern Rhodesia. This dependence obliged Union Minière du Haut Katanga (UMHK), which owned virtually all of the Congo copper mines, to guarantee a certain amount of the copper traffic to Rhodesian railroads.[11] The diversion to Lobito probably resulted from the financial interrelationships among Union Minière, Tanganyika Concessions, Société Génerale de Belgique, the Benguela Railway, and the BCK—as well as UMHK's policy of utilizing all feasible routes as a hedge against the closing of one or more routes for political or other reasons.

In contrast to the success of the national route policy in Northern Rhodesia and in the Congo are the cases of Tanganyika and Angola and their respective railways into Central Africa. The Benguela Railway offers the shortest route from mine to coast for Congo minerals and a route equal in distance with the Beira route for the Northern Rhodesia mines. Terminating on the Atlantic Ocean, it is as much as 2,500 miles closer to the major markets of Europe and North America. Yet the Benguela Railway has never carried a large proportion of Central Africa's copper. None of the rich copper deposits happen to be located in Angola; thus the government has not had the same leverage as have the governments in the Congo and in Northern Rhodesia.

Prior to 1957, no Northern Rhodesia copper moved out through

[11] All of the mining companies have become less dependent on Wankie Coal for power since the opening of the Kariba Dam in 1960 (see Figure 2) and the hydroelectric power stations in the Congo. The coal is still essential, however, for the smelting of copper.

the Angolan route even though the Beira route was overburdened with traffic and the port itself overloaded in the 1950's. The Tripartite Agreement was signed in 1957, providing equal rates to Lobito and Beira and allowing up to 20 percent of the Rhodesian copper to be shipped out on the Benguela Railway. In July 1960, Rhodesia Railways introduced a special discount rate for the last 20 percent of Northern Rhodesia copper being shipped for export. The BCK and the Benguela Railway chose not to meet this new rate, and copper shipments on this route from Northern Rhodesia fell drastically in 1961 and 1962.

Tanganyika, having neither governmental control over mining areas nor any mining interests represented in the ownership of its railway, was in an even worse position than Angola in terms of power to capture copper traffic.

Although Mozambique has no known significant mineral wealth, a large amount of Central African copper has moved on its railways since the turn of the century. BSA was instrumental in the construction and financing of the railway through Mozambique and the port at Beira. In terms of transport, Mozambique was and is essentially an extension of the Rhodesias and the Transvaal because it provides them with ocean ports. Thus, Mozambique railways and ports have traditionally been the recipients of Katanga and Northern Rhodesia copper shipped on the Rhodesia Railways.

Overall, the transport distribution pattern[12] which has emerged from the national route policies of the copper-possessing countries and from various agreements based on political considerations is one of underutilization of the shortest and most economic route to Europe (the Benguela Railway-Lobito route) and possibly overinvestment in Rhodesia Railways and the Mozambique Railways, and in the port of Matadi, the terminal of the Congolese *voie nationale.*

[12] It has been suggested that ocean shipping patterns and rates play a large role in influencing the use of Beira and Lourenço Marques for copper exports. It is true that the present organization of shipping conferences favors the Mozambique ports. This fact is, however, to some extent a result of the allocation of copper among the railways. There is no inherent economic logic to routes or conference structures independent of the traffic offered at particular ports.

CHAPTER II

Implications of Recent
Political Changes

Events of the last five years in South Central Africa have placed severe strains on the historical pattern of rail traffic in the area. It is evident that this pattern will be drastically altered although it is not yet clear what new pattern will emerge.

The event of greatest moment was the breakup of the Federation of Northern Rhodesia, Southern Rhodesia, and Nyasaland and the granting of independence to Zambia. This separated the economy of Zambia (Northern Rhodesia) from that of Rhodesia (Southern Rhodesia) and resulted in several potential sources of trouble: Wankie (Rhodesian) coal, vital to the Zambian copper producers, now lies across a national border; Rhodesia Railways, now jointly owned by Zambia and Rhodesia, may no longer be regarded as the sole national route by Zambia; Rhodesia Railways' present rate policy on copper may well be inimical to Zambian interests; and Zambia is turning to thoughts of additional rail links, in particular to the old idea of a link to the sea through Tanganyika as a means of minimizing its dependence on Rhodesia, the Congo, and Portugal for access to the sea.

The transport implications of the Federation breakup spread, of course, to the Congo and Angola as well as to the east. Rail and port capacities again become matters of concern as each country possessing a port and a rail link (or the potential for one) assesses the likelihood that Zambian copper exports will use its exit.

The present capacity situation presents a mixed picture, in

24

some ways not indicative of the true situation. There is no question but that Rhodesia Railways, using the two Mozambique ports of Beira and Lourenço Marques could handle all of the copper traffic from Zambia and the Congo. The Railways, with minor additions to rolling stock, and the ports with modest improvements, probably could also handle the foreseeable increase in Zambian copper traffic now projected at 800,000 tons by 1970.[1]

However, none of the parties concerned—the Zambian government, the Congolese government, or the copper producers—wishes to commit itself completely to a single rail exit running through three African countries and dependent on a single bridge over the Zambezi River at Victoria Falls.

Only one other exit—the BCK-Benguela route to Lobito—presently could handle more traffic. With additional motive power and rolling stock the capacity of this route could be expanded by one million tons annually inbound and approximately 80-120 thousand tons annually outbound.[2] The present outbound capacity of the Benguela is complicated by three factors:

1. Union Minière copper from Katanga is, in effect, "tied" to manganese ore shipments from the same mining interests. The manganese ore is carried at a low rate, considered by the Benguela to be tolerable so long as this accommodation assures sufficient copper shipments. Manganese shipments now run as high as 300,000 tons annually. This capacity must be recognized as potentially available for higher-rated copper even though it is commercially restricted at present.

2. Angolan production of iron ore in the Cuima[3] area, which has run as high as 500,000 tons per year, is carried by the Benguela to Lobito for export. While the ore is carried at very low rates, the traffic cannot be refused by the Benguela. Present traffic carried is about 300,000 tons per year.

3. New investments in track alignment on the Benguela at the point of escarpment in Angola could increase the outbound ca-

[1] *Economic Survey Mission on the Economic Development of Zambia.* UN /ECA/FAO (Ndola, 1964), p. 44.

[2] London Office, Benguela Railway.

[3] Located some 250 miles inland from Lobito and 50 miles south of the main Benguela Railway line.

pacity by an additional one million tons annually. This improvement—the Cubal Variant—would cost about £5-£8 million.

Neither of the other available exits—through the Congo to Matadi or to Albertville for transshipment across Lake Tanganyika—has spare capacity or economic potential for future expansion. At present both routes have severe problems resulting from neglect and sabotage during the Congo hostilities. Their economic potential is restricted by the necessity for transshipment from rail to water and back to rail.

The route through South Africa is available, but for political and economic reasons it remains unappealing.

The emergence of the Congo as an independent nation in 1960 has had implications for transport policy which are not inconsequential. Perhaps the most important development paving the way for new transport patterns has been the transfer of ownership of the Belgian government's portion of Union Minière shares to the Congolese government. The subsequent increased influence of the Congolese government in mining could well weaken the connection between manganese and copper exports via the Benguela route. This connection, which was evidently useful to the commercial interests of the mining companies, may not be so useful to a Congo government needing to maximize its foreign exchange earnings. Desires to promote the Congolese national route, already manifest, will add yet another pressure on Katanga mining interests and will influence the negotiations of the BCK Railway regarding transit traffic to and from Angola and Zambia. There is no clear indication yet, however, of how the new Congolese government will use its increased power to influence the transport pattern of the area.

Tanganyika[4] also achieved independence during this period, and it has responded favorably to the Zambian idea of a new rail link through its territory to Dar es Salaam. President Nyerere of Tanganyika and President Kaunda of Zambia announced agreement in principle on the building of the rail link on October 16, 1964,[5] although no firm steps have yet been taken by either

[4] Now Tanzania, following the federation of Tanganyika and Zanzibar in 1964. Since we are concerned only with the Tanganyika portion of the federation, we shall continue to use Tanganyika.

[5] *Africa Report,* November 1964, p. 10.

country to finance its construction, estimated to cost upwards of £ 60 million. Even the possibility of this link has repercussions on the transport situation; its actual construction would profoundly affect the distribution of rail traffic in South Central Africa.

A further contributing factor to disturbance of the historical pattern was the initiation by Rhodesia Railways of the discount rate on a part of Zambian copper exports. By this action, which contravened the Tripartite Railway Agreement of equal transit rates to Lobito, Beira, and Lourenço Marques, Rhodesia Railways strengthened the possibility of rate competition.

At the time of this writing, it is not yet clear how the independence crisis in Rhodesia will be resolved. The normal functioning of Rhodesia Railways might well be a casualty of continued political maneuvering.

However, the present crisis in Rhodesia is not the only major political upheaval which can be expected in South Central Africa over the next few years. Speculation on what may happen is not, therefore, a very productive enterprise. Some analysis of what *ought* to happen, based on more fundamental and long-range goals of economic development, may be more to the point. The chapters which follow attempt to isolate three key elements for this analysis: improvements in the utilization of existing rail facilities, pricing policy on rail freight, and decisions on new rail investment.

CHAPTER III

Improving the Utilization
of Rail Facilities

MORE EFFICIENT UTILIZATION of existing rail
facilities is critical to the establishment of a rational distribution
of freight traffic in South Central Africa. A number of factors are
now hindering efficient utilization, among them the Tripartite
Agreement; the railway agreement[1] between Zambia and Rhodesia negotiated at the time of the Federation breakup; the resurgence of *voie nationale* as a transport policy in the Congo, and
the Beira Convention. If changes could be made in these institutional arrangements, the resulting improvement could well ob-
viate any necessity for new rail investment for the foreseeable future.

Tripartite Agreement

It is difficult to find justification for continuing any portion of
this agreement, which restricts the amount of Zambian copper
which may go out through Lobito and equalizes copper rates
from the Zambian copperbelt stations to Lobito, Beira, and
Lourenço Marques. Rhodesia Railways have already abrogated
the second feature of the Agreement through the initiation of the
special discount rate on copper. Zambia needs to be able to exer-

[1] "Agreement between the Government of Southern Rhodesia and the Government of Northern Rhodesia Relating to the Rhodesia Railways," *Southern Rhodesia
Government Gazette*, Vol. XLI, No. 56 (Salisbury, 1963). For text see Appendix C.

cise full discretion on routing of all its traffic, both in and outbound; this discretion is now limited by the Agreement.

Allowing the Agreement to lapse would, in conjunction with other changes discussed below, create the following possibilities:

1. Zambia would be free to utilize the Lobito exit without restriction.

2. All the railways would be free to make new rates on transit freight which reflect their own cost and service characteristics. Thus, the Benguela, which can offer faster service to and from Zambia, could reflect this advantage in its rate structure. The Rhodesia Railways, which may have a cost advantage because of its two-way traffic to the copper stations (coal inbound, copper outbound) could reflect its advantage in lower rates.

3. Both the Congo and Zambia would have several rail exits to choose from, providing differences in speed and cost of shipment but sufficiently alike to allow competition for their shipments and thus minimize the possibilities of exhorbitant rates being charged by either railway.

4. Making use of competing railways, neither the Congolese Government nor the Zambian Government would have any great need for investment in new rail facilities.

None of the preceding four possibilities will come into being simply because the Tripartite Agreement is allowed to lapse. Other changes are also needed.

The Zambia-Rhodesia Agreement

While the Tripartite Agreement restricts Zambian use of the Lobito exit, the Zambia-Rhodesia Agreement, arranging joint ownership of Rhodesia Railways, restricts Zambian use of *any* exit other than those provided by Rhodesia Railways. Moreover, the Agreement ties Zambia to the rate structure presently in force on Rhodesia Railways.

The Agreement, reluctantly entered into by Zambia prior to independence, provides that compensation be paid to the Railways—by either country (Zambia or Rhodesia) whenever a diversion of traffic occurs because of unilateral action by that country—in an amount equal to the revenues lost by Rhodesia Railways; and recognizes that the Railways will apply "a commercially sound rating structure," a value-of-service rating structure designed to insure the financial solvency of the Railways. The effect of the latter provision on Zambia will be discussed in the next chapter.

The compensation provision, while it applies to both countries, is operative only in the case of Zambia since Rhodesia has no economic alternative to using the Railways. It may be argued that Zambia has no economic alternative either since, as half owner of the Railways, Zambia is liable for half of any deficit on the Railways resulting from diversion of traffic. The BCK-Benguela route, with modest improvements and additions to rolling stock, could provide an economic alternative for Zambia.

It is quite possible that cases will occur (for example, where speed of service is important) in which the economic gain to be realized from Zambian use of the alternate route of Lobito would outweigh the loss of revenues on Rhodesia Railways and possible resulting deficit. Were such cases to persist there would be reason to consider contraction of service on Rhodesia Railways and even some disinvestment. Such "signals," however, cannot be perceived if the compensation principle is maintained because compensation payments do not reflect economic cost. These payments are designed solely to insure financial solvency of Rhodesia Railways at a given size, rate structure, and organization— none of which may be efficient now or at any point in the future.

It is widely recognized that the Railways Agreement, drawn up rather hastily because of the necessity to apportion its debt between Zambia and Rhodesia when the Federation was dissolved, is not a perfect instrument. The Agreement did keep the Railways operating under a single management, and it is in both countries' interest that it continue so. Adjustments of the Agreement, which will be necessary from time to time, should be focused on improving the chances for continued operation as a single unit. The question of Zambian traffic diversion is one, we suggest, which must be re-examined in that light.

Resurgence of *Voie Nationale* in the Congo

The resurgence[2] of a national route policy in the Congo is a second potential obstacle to efficient utilization of existing rail facilities. The route's natural disadvantages (length of route, time, and cost of transshipment) are sufficient, moreover, to call into question the long-term usefulness of the route for mineral traffic from Katanga. The BCK railway, which serves as a link in both the Matadi and Lobito routes, might well concentrate on Lobito for mineral exports. On this route no transshipment is required; the rail cars can go straight through to Lobito without unloading and reloading. To be sure, foreign exchange is required to pay a portion of the freight bill on the Lobito route (that portion accruing to the Benguela) and foreign exchange is, at the moment, a vexing problem for the Congo. Prior to independence, however, the Congo was a net foreign exchange earner for Belgium. In the longer run Congolese mineral and agricultural exports should place the Congo once again in a relatively good foreign exchange position, presuming the products are not burdened with higher transport costs than they need be. The former Belgian transport policy was one of inducing use of the national route through Matadi by a variety of means, including lower rates than those in force via Lobito. Such a policy, encouraging the use of an existing route, has economic logic so long as the costs incurred are lower than the costs of using an alternate route. Because Congolese exports are sold at world prices and inefficiencies of production and transport cannot be passed along to buyers in the form of higher export prices, it is difficult to hold out much hope that the national route can meet the "lower cost" criterion.

---

[2] Provisional figures for 1964 show that over 81,000 metric tons of copper moved through Matadi. This contrasts with some 12,000 tons in 1963 (see Table 2) and indicates both physical reconstruction of the line as well as the renewed pressure on Union Minière to use this exit.

The Beira Convention[3]

The Convention, which guarantees Zambian and Rhodesian traffic to Beira, may be said to be one of the prime reasons why the Zambia-Rhodesia Railways agreement of 1963 focused so heavily on the question of traffic diversion. So long as the Convention remains in effect, Rhodesia Railways are obligated to utilize the Mozambique exit to the fullest extent possible and are prevented from altering any freight rate if the alteration has the effect of diverting traffic from this exit.

The criticisms of the Railways Agreement apply, therefore, with equal force to the continuation of this Convention. Zambia does not have the same geographical tie to Mozambique which Rhodesia has. Situated more nearly in the center of Africa from an east-west standpoint, Zambia can profitably utilize both coasts for its imports and exports. Rhodesia has no such opportunity. The Convention, drawn up when both countries were considered one, now operates as a restriction upon Zambian freedom of choice on its transit traffic.

The Real Problem of Transit Traffic

The problem of obtaining freedom of access to the sea has faced landlocked countries for centuries. It has contributed to the starting of wars and the reformation of national boundaries. It is natural that the colonial powers occupied themselves with treaties, agreements, and uneconomic transport investment to insure access to the sea from Central Africa. The presence of valuable minerals far inland added to the incentive. The legacy of investment and agreements are now, however, ill suited to the needs of the new countries who possess the mineral wealth, Zambia and the Congo.

Fortunately, an alternative to the continuation of the present

[3] See Appendix B for text.

agreements and policies of *voie nationale* now exists. Recognizing that the problem of transit traffic is common to all landlocked nations, a United Nations committee has recently proposed a Draft Convention Relating to Transit Trade of Landlocked Countries.[4] Organized under the auspices of the 1964 UN Conference on Trade and Development, the committee includes members from most of the world's landlocked countries. The draft convention is designed to facilitate transit trade and contains provisions which would make it unnecessary for each landlocked country to bargain with its neighbors for access to the sea. These provisions include: (1) freedom of transit without discrimination; (2) restrictions on customs duties and transit fees other than for administration; (3) guarantees of reasonable tariffs (rates) and adequate transport services in the "transit" states.

Were such a general convention as this to be adopted, giving landlocked countries the use of transit facilities and ports as a matter of *right,* it would greatly reduce the dangers resulting from the use of transport for political purposes. If the framework for a regional, nonpolitical approach to transport in South Central Africa were already established (either through the UN Convention or some similar regional agreement), the possibility of Rhodesia Railways being split at the Zambian border would not even exist. Such an arrangement would also reduce the political necessity for new transport investment, in particular the Zambian-Tanganyikan rail link and major reinvestment in some of the Congo lines. As the country most seriously affected by the present bilateral and trilateral agreements, Zambia should take the lead in pressing for the adoption of an international solution.

[4] *United Nations Monthly Chronicle,* Vol. 1, No. 7 (December 1964), pp. 40-41.

CHAPTER IV

Rail Pricing Policy

THE MOST CONCISE statement of the philosophy of pricing on the railways in South Central Africa is given in the 1959 Harragin Report on Rhodesia Railways:

> . . . the broad principles of railway rating should be such as to secure no lower revenue from any particular traffic than the direct cost of carrying it and . . . the burden of overhead costs should be distributed over the total traffic of the system in accordance with the ability of each traffic to pay.[1]

The accurate application of these principles should result in a system of rates geared, on a commodity-by-commodity basis, to the price and time elasticities of demand for transport services. Such a system is known commonly as a price discrimination or value-of-service rate system.[2]

In practice the value-of-service rate system departs from strict price discrimination. Commodities are grouped in a manageable number of categories for rating purposes even though their individual elasticities may differ. Rates are changed infrequently; rarely more than once a year and often not for several years. For convenience and reasons of "equity," some rate changes are "across-the-board" percentage changes which obviously violate the concept of the perfectly discriminating monopolist.

---

[1] "Report of the Commission of Inquiry into the Rating Structure of the Rhodesia Railways," Federation of Rhodesia and Nyasaland (Salisbury, 1959), p. 9.

[2] For a general discussion of railway price discrimination, see John R. Meyer et al., The Economics of Competition in the Transportation Industries (Harvard University Press, 1960), pp. 170 ff., and George W. Wilson, Essays on Some Unsettled Questions in the Economics of Transportation (Foundation for Business and Economic Studies, Indiana University, 1962), pp. 152 ff.

In general, however, the value-of-service rate system operates by charging less than average cost on some commodities and charging more than average cost on other commodities. The rate differentials may be as much as 10 to 1; a commodity with highly elastic demand characteristics may have a rate of only one-tenth that of another commodity whose demand characteristics are highly inelastic. The direct costs of moving the two commodities may be exactly the same. No rate is less than the direct or marginal shipping cost.

This system of rates is designed, as is the less efficient system of average cost pricing, to keep the railway self-supporting, to recover all costs from the transport users. Whether it does depends heavily upon four major factors:

1. The technical efficiency or the cost characteristics of the railway. This involves its alignment, equipment, and operating efficiency.

2. The quantity, value, and elasticities of demand of the commodities carried.

3. The absence or presence of alternative carriers or substitutes for transport which may change the demand for rail service.

4. The railways debt position and capital structure.

In terms of rail traffic alone, it can be said that the value-of-service rate system has produced revenues more than sufficient to cover operating costs on the three railways with which we are most concerned—the BCK, the Benguela, and Rhodesia Railways. On average and abstracting from recent disruptions of traffic on the BCK, the annual surplus from railway working accounts is estimated as follows:[3]

BCK	£3,200,000
Benguela	£3,000,000
Rhodesia Railways	£3,500,000

When account is taken of nonoperating costs, including interest and repayment charges on debt, the comparable estimates on annual profit are:[4]

[3] Based on annual reports for the period 1959-63, corrected for abnormal and nonrecurring variations.

[4] *Ibid.*

BCK	£ 750,000
Benguela	£2,000,000
Rhodesia Railways	£ 500,000

These figures describe a period when all three railways were operating fairly close to capacity in one direction with existing rolling stock—Rhodesia Railways inbound and the BCK-Benguela outbound. In terms of the four major factors just referred to, these figures reflect:

1. A reasonable technical efficiency with few of the anachronisms found in the rail systems of many underdeveloped countries. For example, total costs on a ton-mile basis for all three railways fall between 1.5d and 1.8d, or close to 2 U.S. cents per ton-mile at present traffic levels. This compares not unfavorably with total ton-mile costs by rail in the United States and Western Europe.

2. The existence of traffic, chiefly imported manufactured goods and copper exports, which can bear a relatively high freight rate.

3. The absence of price competition by trucks. In Zambia and Rhodesia there is a formal agreement with truck operators which forbids price competition. In the Congo and Angola no truck industry of any magnitude yet exists.

4. Debt positions which do not negate the first three advantages.

In addition, it should be recalled that present agreements restrict price competition by the railways in those areas, chiefly Zambia, where more than one rail route could effectively be used.

Implications of the Present Pricing Policy

A properly managed value-of-service rate system has some important economic implications in addition to its financial self-support abilities. It approximates a marginal cost pricing system in terms of utilization of existing facilites. No traffic which can bear a rate equal to the marginal cost of carrying it will be driven away. Rate adjustments will not, of course, be instantaneous or absolutely precise but neither, in actual operation, would the marginal cost pricing adjustments. In the utilization aspect the system is consonant with larger goals of national economic development.

The influence on location of industry exerted by a value-of-service system should also approximate that of the marginal cost pricing system, although it is not certain to do so in practice. Elements of bargaining between the railway and the industry would almost certainly intrude in the location decision. The precision of the information held by both sides in the bargaining process would determine how close the approximation comes.

Other implications of value-of-service pricing have more complex relationships to the goals of economic development, and these must be looked at in more detail. They include: rail operating efficiency; viability of the rate system; effect on size of the railway investment; effect on investment in other sectors of the economy; and national economies vs. international railways.

However, it is first necessary to examine the degree to which the value-of-service pricing system is actually pursued by the three railways. In theory, a fully discriminating monopolist would be concerned with profit maximization and would charge rates which insure the highest profit. This calculation would take into account possible alternatives open to the shipper, including the possibility of developing another means of shipment. In practice, the railways must take political as well as economic possibilities into their calculations. Moreover, in the case of the government-owned Rhodesia Railways, the goal is not profit maximization but simply financial self-sufficiency and a rate-of-return position which is attractive in the international capital market. The BCK, a "mixed" company with both governmental and private stockholders, cannot pursue a purely profit-maximizing policy. The Benguela, although almost wholly in private hands, must gauge the political realities of its profit motives and must, in particular circumstances, charge rates on local Angolan goods which are less than a pure price discrimination policy would prescribe.

In the discussion which follows, it is the pricing system as practiced by the three railways which is reviewed. Rhodesia Railways examples are used almost exclusively, both because data are available and because Rhodesia Railways policy and Zambian

TABLE 4. *Rhodesia Railways Copper Tonnage and Revenue in Relation to Total Rail Tonnage and Revenue, 1950–63*[a]
(Tonnage in short tons)

	Copper Tonnage (1,000)	Total Freight Tons (1,000)	Copper Tonnage as Percentage of Total Freight Tonnage	Copper Revenue (£1,000)	Total Rail Revenue (£1,000)	Copper Revenue as Percentage of Total Revenue	Copper Price (£ per long ton)
1950	341.3	5,755.2	5.9	1,010.4	9,955.2	10.1	179.0
1951	377.1	6,689.3	5.6	1,358.1	11,960.2	11.4	220.7
1952	419.1	7,296.4	5.7	1,638.4	13,115.2	12.5	259.5
1953	420.9	7,894.8	5.3	1,714.9	15,628.0	11.0	256.3
1954	507.0	8,615.2	5.9	2,155.6	17,383.9	12.4	249.3
1955	463.9	9,106.5	5.1	2,833.1	21,161.2	13.4	351.7
1956	511.3	10,065.1	5.1	3,174.8	23,540.8	13.5	328.7
1957	580.2	11,250.7	5.2	4,945.9	27,191.7	18.2	219.4
1958	639.6	12,024.3	5.3	8,153.9	36,591.0	22.3	197.7
1959	697.5	11,159.5	6.3	5,866.6	26,603.3	22.1	237.7
1960	905.9	12,179.5	7.4	7,760.2	31,357.1	24.7	245.8
1961	1,024.8	12,242.1	8.4	8,783.8	32,127.5	27.3	229.7
1962	977.3	11,992.3	8.1	8,312.0	30,921.0	26.9	234.0
1963	947.6	11,630.3	8.1	8,868.6	32,175.4	27.6	234.4

Source: Rhodesia Railways, *Annual Reports*, 1953–63 and *Northern Rhodesia Chamber of Mines Yearbook*, 1963.

[a] Prior to 1958, Rhodesia Railways operated on a fiscal year from April 1 through March 31. Beginning in 1958, the fiscal year was changed to terminate on June 30. Therefore, the 1958 figures include railway tonnage and revenues generated for a fifteen-month period from April 1, 1957 to June 30, 1958.

policy are pivotal to the rail pricing problem in South Central Africa.

Rail Operating Efficiency. In the absence of a strong competitive situation there is no assurance that any pricing policy will make for efficient operations. A value-of-service policy has obvious weaknesses in this regard which are particularly relevant in South Central Africa. Two major categories of traffic—imported manufactured goods and high-value copper exports—can and do bear substantial tariffs on all three railways. When there is a serious drop in earnings on the railways, the tendency is to make it up by increasing the rates on these commodities rather than looking too hard at possible cost reductions. The rise in copper revenues on Rhodesia Railways in the 1950's, shown in Table 4, illustrates this tendency. Where cost reductions involve a cut in the labor force, political considerations will reinforce this tendency. The result is an inherent bias against efficiency when profit maximization is absent. It is only when overall deficits occur, as was the case on Rhodesia Railways during the past two years—£607,000 in 1961-62, and £741,713 for 1962-63—that cost reduction incentives begin to appear and actions to reduce costs are taken.

Viability of the Rate System. A value-of-service rate system depends upon a substantial degree of monopoly power in the hands of the railways. It is demonstrable that in Africa[5], as elsewhere, the coming of roads and trucks will undermine that power. Even though Rhodesia Railways' agreement with the Long-Distance Truck Operators, which restricts direct price competition on rail routes, was renewed in 1963, it cannot be expected to do more than delay the time when high-rated goods susceptible to truck movement will move by truck. As such traffic is lost, or retained by lowering rates on that traffic, more of the burden of overhead costs (which will not shrink proportionally) will be thrown onto traffic which cannot move economically by truck. Copper will then figure even more importantly than at present as a bearer of

[5] Sir James Farquharson, "The Role of Railways in Developing Countries," in Papers Presented at a Conference on Civil Engineering Problems Overseas (London: Institution of Civil Engineers, 1962), pp. 150-51.

the overhead costs. Direct competition by the three railways for copper could eventually destroy much of the profitability of that traffic.

The process of erosion of the railways' ability to use price discrimination will probably be speeded up as economic development accelerates. Restrictions designed to delay the process by suppressing investment in alternative transport services may achieve financial self-sufficiency at the expense of further economic progress. That the process of erosion is present in South Central Africa is evident by the agreements previously mentioned which aim at preserving monopoly power by writ where it has been lost in fact; and, paradoxically, by the violation of one such agreement—the discount rate on copper instituted by Rhodesia Railways in 1960—to recapture copper going out through Lobito.

Effect on Size of Rail Investment. Railway use of a value-of-service rate system may, under certain circumstances, promote overinvestment in railway facilities. The circumstances which have been present particularly in the Rhodesia Railways case include: (1) rail investment policy which is not coordinated with overall national investment policy; (2) substantial tonnage of high-value commodities which can bear a high freight rate and whose cost of shipment is low, resulting in large realizable surplus for a railway from their shipment; (3) political pressures to expand rail service; (4) the lack of or containment of competitive forces; (5) a policy of self-sufficiency instead of profit maximization; and (6) inability of other sectors of the economy to price their products in a value-of-service fashion—they sell at the same price to all buyers.

With these factors present, a railway may violate its own rule of "not charging less for any traffic than the direct costs of hauling it" and generate uneconomic traffic so long as the surplus from its lucrative traffic keeps net earnings in the black. For example, the Harragin Commission Report[6] cites passenger rates and distribution rates on many commodities as cases of Rhodesia Railways rates prior to 1960 which were lower than their direct haulage costs. Branch lines whose revenue potential is not

[6] *Op. cit.*, pp. 58, 68.

sufficient to cover direct costs, with or without interest charges, may result from this situation.

Even if the railway does not violate its rule on marginal traffic, it is still possible that overinvestment will occur relative to investment in other sectors. This may be simply because the user revenues are more easily visualized than are returns from investments in, say, education, or because, as a generator of surplus funds, the railway can invest closer to the margin than can most other sectors in capital-short countries.

Effect on Investment in Other Sectors of the Economy. The effects of railway value-of-service pricing on other sectors of the economy are pervasive and may well be detrimental. Transport costs enter into the production of almost all goods. To the extent that these costs are higher than the cost of providing them, distortions are created, and misallocation of resources occurs. For example, if two commodities are charged different rates while the cost of carrying them is the same, the tendency, when other conditions are the same, is for investment to be higher in one and lower in the other than would otherwise be the case. Regional variations in investment may also be affected if price discrimination follows a regional pattern. Railway rates have often been deliberately patterned by governments to minimize regional variation in incomes and investment.

In South Central Africa governmental policies have in general been well served by the value-of-service rate system. Low rates encourage agricultural development and allow exploitation of low-value mineral resources. High rates on imports act as a restraint on the use of foreign exchange and high rates on high-valued minerals (produced by foreign investors) capture a share of investor profits.

Even with this apparent identity of interests, serious problems arise in connection with rates on high-valued minerals. The copper case in Zambia is again used to illustrate these problems, one of which relates to *who* captures the share of investor profits. This problem is treated in the next section.

The other problem is the effect of a high copper freight rate on taxation of the copper mining companies. Table 4 indicates the rise of copper revenues relative to total freight revenues on Rhodesia Railways and shows that this rise is rather independent of the increase in copper tonnage or of copper prices. By 1956, Sir Ernest Oppenheimer, head of Anglo-American Corporation,[7] was warning:

> We are inclined to think, for instance, that the recent increase in railway rates on copper verges on being an unsound method of raising funds, as it seems to introduce a discriminatory tariff *for purposes that go beyond the ordinary revenue requirements of the railway* . . . the mines are being called upon to subsidize the unprofitable sections of the railways *and to provide capital funds out of revenue* . . . *the new rates will clearly be an important factor in determining the profitability or otherwise of other, smaller copper mining ventures.* . . .[8]

It is not remarkable to find a shipper protesting an increase in rates and predicting that unfortunate consequences for all will follow from the increase. What the statement points up, however, is the relationship among the value-of-service rate on copper, general taxation of copper profits, and marginal mines. Costs of producing copper in Zambia compare favorably overall with other world producers, being on the order of £160 per long ton delivered in Europe.[9] Total transport costs accounted in 1963 for some 14 percent (£22.4 per long ton) of this cost[10] with the rail charge responsible for some £17 of the cost per long ton. While we may discount the Oppenheimer statement as it related to 1956, the rate increases since that time and the strong emphasis of the Zambian government on future increases in copper production (and corresponding increases in government revenues from taxation of profits or direct sharing of profits) make the statement more relevant today. The 1962 Zambian copper production of

---

[7] One of the two major copper mining companies in Zambia, the other being Roan Selection Trust (RST).

[8] Quoted in *The Mining Journal* (Nov. 23, 1956), p. 620. Emphasis added.

[9] *Economic Survey Mission on the Economic Development of Zambia, op. cit.,* p. 42. Note, however, that individual mine costs vary widely. According to Sir Ronald Prain, quoted in *The Mining Journal* (Dec. 18, 1964), p. 465, there is a spread of £100 per ton in the cost, due mainly to variations in the grade of copper ore.

[10] *Northern Rhodesia Chamber of Mines Yearbook* (1963), p. 28.

603,000 short tons was achieved with the mines being worked at about 85 percent of capacity. An increase to full capacity of present investment will not produce the 800,000 to 825,000 short tons projected by the United Nations Survey Mission and desired by the Zambian government. New investment, including new mines, will be needed. Yet the rail rates in effect at present are judged[11] to be as high as the present mines can bear and too high to warrant bringing any less profitable mines into operation. This judgment is borne out by Rhodesia Railways' shift to cost reductions instead of increases in rates[12] as a method of overcoming its deficits of 1962 and 1963.

At the present time copper prices are well above 1962-63 levels and thus the above constraints do not seem too worrisome. Neither the copper producers nor the United Nations Survey Mission expect, or desire, this price level to persist[13] since use of substitutes for copper as well as development of new copper capacity elsewhere would probably more than offset the benefit of high prices.

The lack of coordination between the Zambian government in its planning for tax revenues and Rhodesia Railways and its rate levels thus becomes a real issue. The point seems to be reached where the present freight rates on high-valued commodities (in particular copper and imports) can in the future, if they do not do so now, adversely affect the ability of the copper producers to expand and thus to pay taxes on the profits of that expansion. The implications of this problem are far-reaching and emphasize the distortions in the value-of-service price mechanism as it is now practiced.

These implications may be examined by dealing with two objections which may be brought against posing the problem in the terms just stated. First, the problem does not arise because the railway has mistaken the elasticity of demand for transport by the copper producers and thus violated its second rule—dis-

[11] Conversations with Roan Selection Trust officials in November 1963.

[12] Either on imported machinery or on copper since both are relevant to the costs of opening a new mine.

[13] *Economic Survey Mission on the Economic Development of Zambia, op. cit.,* p. 45.

tributing overhead costs in accordance with the ability of each traffic to pay. The problem arises because, in the case of copper, the railway has utilized the limit of the present elasticity which is high and captured the maximum amount *for the railway,* impairing the ability of Zambia to capture more than it does at present in direct taxation from the copper producers.[14] More important, however, the size of the Railways' overhead costs, which have been supported by high copper rates, may act as a constraint on investment in new copper production, since the new mines would be higher-cost mines, unable to bear the high copper rate.

The second objection goes as follows: Since Rhodesia Railways are government-owned, what difference does it make whether the copper producers are "taxed" through rail rates or directly on profits? Besides the difference just noted—distortion in investment in nontransport sectors of the economy—there is another difference. To the extent that railway surpluses do not go into a general revenue account (and what railway would have surpluses if they did?), the railway "tax" is an earmarked tax and suffers from all the disabilities of earmarked taxes. In this connection it is worth recording that both Roan Selection Trust and Anglo-American officials have indicated a basic tolerance of high freight rates precisely because they go to the railway, and an antipathy to increased profit taxation, the proceeds of which might be used for any governmental purpose. Governmental revenues, however, must remain an allocation prerogative of governments, not of private companies. Zambia does not at present have that prerogative.

National Economies Versus International Railways. The final implication of a value-of-service rate system relates specifically

---

[14] One should note that this tax, averaging 40 percent of company profits, is "relatively mild." See page 42 of the U.N. Survey previously cited. Zambia revenues from copper will also increase substantially because of its taking over the royalties on copper formerly paid to BSA. The royalty payment settlement relieves the Zambian government from any pressing need to increase the tax rate on copper producers but does not change the argument relative to freight rates. The present formula for calculating the royalty payment is based on the price of copper rather than on company profits. This also raises questions about production levels attainable and marginal mines.

to the political boundaries in South Central Africa and does not have general applicability.[15] We have tried to show in the preceding section that a value-of-service system may result in overinvestment in railways relative to other sectors of the economy. If the railway serves more than one country and if it happens that the high-valued commodities are preponderantly in one country, the income transfers and misallocations cut across national boundaries and involve losses to one national economy and gains to the other.

The case is illustrated at the present time by Zambia and Rhodesia and the jointly owned Rhodesia Railways. Table 5 gives revenue per ton for major commodities hauled by Rhodesia Railways in the year ending June 30, 1963. Copper revenues have been broken down into their component parts so that they can be compared to other traffic. Unless the general goods category, which includes a number of high-valued imports as well as low-valued goods, disguises a large contrary trend (which is not likely in terms of the pattern of trade of the two countries), it is clear that Zambian traffic produced markedly higher revenues per ton and per ton-mile than did Rhodesian traffic. This is more sharply pointed up in Tables 6, 7, and 8, which estimate profit or loss on each principal commodity.

Since it may not be immediately obvious why three sets of cost estimates are included, some explanation of these is in order. The crudest estimate of fully distributed costs[16] is made by using railway working expenses plus debt service costs and net ton-miles produced by the railway. The resulting cost per ton-mile of 1.57 pence was developed on this basis. The precision of this figure is largely irrelevant to this discussion which is interested not in absolute costs but in relative costs of carrying each commodity. This 1.57 pence figure was used as the basis of cost estimates in column 1 of Tables 6, 7, and 8. Comparisons of the cost of individual commodities using an *average* ton-mile cost will be inaccurate. At the very least, two components of cost—terminal

[15] It is applicable to some other specific cases, notably the East Africa situation, in which one railway serves three countries.

[16] Implicit in using fully distributed costs is acceptance of the fact that Rhodesia Railways will continue to pursue a financial self-sufficiency policy.

TABLE 5. Rhodesia Railways Goods Traffic, Tonnage and Revenue, July 1, 1962–June 30, 1963

(Tonnage in short tons)

Commodity	Tonnage Hauled	Revenue (£)	Revenue per Ton (£)	Average Length of Haul (miles)	Average Revenue per Ton-mile (pence)	Estimated Product Valuation per Ton (£)	Product Origin
General Goods[a]	4,890,774	15,140,869.0	3.10	396	1.90	n.a.[b]	Zambia and Rhodesia
(Tobacco)	(171,780)	(358,742.0)	2.09	170	2.95	347	Mostly Rhodesia
(Maize and maize meal)	(650,836)	(549,225.0)	0.84	175	1.15	15	Mostly Rhodesia
Asbestos	139,128	215,951.0	1.55	213	1.65	42	Rhodesia
Chrome Ore	393,293	270,949.0	0.69	213–297	0.47	5	Rhodesia
Copper (total)	933,489	8,590,137.3[c]				210	
ZAMBIA (total)	591,721	7,312,336.8					Zambia
Full Rate	473,912	6,144,866.5					
To Beira	202,574	2,800,482.5	13.82	1,259	2.60		
To Lourenço-Marques	271,338	3,344,384.0	12.33	1,122	2.60		
Discount Rate	94,127	803,610.0					
To Beira	43,700	395,659.8	9.05	1,259	1.70		
To Lourenço-Marques	50,427	407,950.2	8.09	1,122	1.70		
To South African Republic	23,682	363,860.3	15.36	1,257	2.90		
CONGO (total)	93,780	1,277,800.5					Congo
To Beira (first 70,000 tons)	70,000	983,008.6	14.04	1,269	2.60		
To Beira (after 70,000 tons)	20,065	238,372.2	11.90				
To South African Republic	3,715	56,419.7	15.18	1,267	2.90		

Other Minerals	1,664,652	1,122,501.0	0.67	n.a.	n.a.	n.a.	n.a.
Livestock	212,406	312,977.0	1.47	160	2.21	13.5	Mostly Rhodesia
Coal and Coke	2,164,487	2,903,087.0	1.34	460	.70	1.0	Rhodesia
TOTAL	10,492,292	29,848,195.0					

Sources: Tonnage and revenue figures for all commodities except copper are from Rhodesia Railways *Annual Report for Year Ending June 30, 1963*. Copper revenue figures for Zambian copper destined for Mozambique ports based on rates set by Tripartite Agreement (see text). Prior to September 1962, the full through rate to Beira and Lourenço-Marques from Ndola was £14.17.10. No copper was hauled at special discount rates in July and August. (Note that revenues are shared by Rhodesia Railways and Mozambique Railways on a pro rata basis.) Special rate for Zambian copper to Republic of South Africa (Ndola to Ramatlhabama) was 282.3 shillings per ton. Through rate for Congo copper to Beira (from Congo Border Station) was 302.55 shillings per ton on the first 70,000 tons. Through rate for Congo copper from Congo Border Station to Ramatlhabama was 282.4 shillings per ton. As of September 1, 1962, Rhodesia Railways raised rates on all goods traffic by 10 percent. From that date, the above rates were: Zambian copper: full through rate to Mozambique ports—£16.6.8; special discount rate to Ramatlhabama—310.5 shillings. Congo copper: through rate to Beira—332.8 shillings per ton for first 70,000 tons; 275 shillings per ton for any tonnage in excess of 70,000 tons; through rate to Ramatlhabama—312.6 shillings per ton. Note that all copper rates quoted for Zambian copper are based on assumption that Ndola is point of origin. Actually, shipments originate from many Copperbelt stations, and rates vary slightly from the Ndola rate. Tonnage figures are based on data supplied by Roan Selection Trust, Ltd. (Salisbury and Lusaka Offices). Average length of haul figures: Figure for "General Goods" from Rhodesia Railways *Annual Report for Year Ending June 30, 1963*. Copper, lead, zinc, asbestos, and chrome ore are based on calculations of distances from points of origin (location of mines) to points of destination. Other figures are from *Report of the Commission of Inquiry Into the Rating Structure of the Rhodesia Railways* (Salisbury, 1959). Product valuation figures: Values for copper, lead, and zinc are based on figures in Northern Rhodesian Chamber of Mines *Year Book 1963*, Kitwe, Zambia, 1964. Maize and livestock figures are based on information in Northern Rhodesia, *Monthly Digest of Statistics*, Issue No. 7, October 1964, Central Statistical Office, Lusaka. Tobacco, asbestos, chrome ore and coal and coke figures are from *Overseas Survey 1964*, Barclays Bank, Ltd., London.

a "Tobacco" and "Maize and maize meal" are components of the "General Goods" category. Figures for these two subcategories which are contained in the "General Goods" figures are in parentheses.

b n.a.=not available.

c The total revenue for copper railings given in Rhodesia Railways *Annual Report for Year Ending June 30, 1963* is £8,868,643. The difference between this figure and the total here of £8,590,187.3 may be assumed to be revenue earned from local railings.

TABLE 6. *Estimated Profit or Loss of Principal Traffics on Rhodesia Railways, 200 Mile Equal Point*

(Tonnage in short tons)

(July 1, 1962–June 30, 1963)

Principal Categories of Traffic	Cost per Ton[a] (£)	Cost per Ton[b]			Revenue per Ton[e] (£)	Profit or Loss per Ton (£)	PROFIT or LOSS (on total tonnage carried of each traffic) (£)	Product Origin
		Terminal	+ Line Haul =	Total (£)				
General Goods[d]	2.59	.87	+ 1.72 =	2.59	3.10	+ .51	2,494,294.74	Zambia and Rhodesia
(Tobacco)	1.11	.87	+ .74 =	1.61	2.09	+ .48	(82,454.40)	Mostly Rhodesia
(Maize and maize meal)	1.14	.87	+ .76 =	1.63	0.84	− .79	(514,160.44)	Mostly Rhodesia
Asbestos	1.47	.87	+ .92 =	1.79	1.55	− .24	33,390.72	Rhodesia
Chrome ore	2.29	.87	+ 1.11 =	1.98	0.69	−1.29	507,347.97	Rhodesia
Copper[e]								
ZAMBIA								
Full Rate								
Beira	8.24	.87	+ 5.46 =	6.33	13.82	+7.49	1,517,279.26	
Lourenço-Marques	7.34	.87	+ 4.86 =	5.73	12.33	+6.60	1,790,830.80	
Discount Rate								
Beira	8.24	.87	+ 5.46 =	6.33	9.05	+2.72	118,864.00	Zambia
Lourenço-Marques	7.34	.87	+ 4.86 =	5.73	8.09	+2.36	119,007.72	
To South African								

tons)	8.30	.87 + 5.50 = 6.37	14.04	+7.67	536,900.00	
Beira (excess of 70,000 tons)	8.30	.87 + 5.50 = 6.37	11.90	+5.53	110,959.45	Congo
To South African Republic	8.29	.87 + 5.49 = 6.36	15.18	+8.82	32,376.30	
LOCAL RAILINGS	n.a.	n.a.	n.a.	n.a.	n.a.	
Zinc and Lead	7.44	.87 + 4.93 = 5.80	6.42	+.62	49,554.74	Zambia
Other Minerals	n.a.	n.a.	0.67	n.a.	n.a.	
Livestock	1.05	.87 + .69 = 1.56	1.47	−.09	19,116.54	Mostly Rhodesia
Coal and coke	3.01	.87 + 1.99 = 2.86	1.34	−1.52	3,290,020.24	Rhodesia

a These cost figures are based on a working figure of 1.57 pence per ton-mile as the average fully allocated cost per ton-mile.

b These cost figures are calculated on the basis of a constant terminal cost independent of distance plus an average line-haul cost per ton-mile. Using the average ton-mile cost of 1.57 pence and an average haul of 396 miles, terminal costs were calculated as follows: $K + 396y = 621.72$ pence, where K is the terminal cost and y the line haul ton-mile cost. K was then successively set equal to 100 y, 150 y, and 200 y in order to obtain three estimates of average terminal costs and average line haul costs. United States experience indicates a value closer to 100 y for K, while African railways, with smaller tonnage cars, would more likely be closer to the 200 y figure.

c Revenue figures on individual traffics with the exception of copper are derived from Rhodesia Railways *Annual Report for Year Ending June 30, 1963*. For derivation of copper revenue per ton figures, see footnote to Table 5.

d "Tobacco" and "Maize and maize meal" are components of "General Goods" category. Figures for these two subcategories which are contained in "General Goods" figures are in parentheses.

e Copper figures are broken down because costs and revenues vary (and therefore profits and losses) according to differences in length of haul and in rates. Full rate for Zambian copper destined for Beira and Lourenço-Marques is £16.6.8 per ton. Discount rate for Zambian copper to these ports is £10.9.7. Revenues are shared by Rhodesia Railways and Mozambique Railways on a pro rata basis. Source of rates for Zambian copper to Republic of South Africa and Congo copper to Beira and Republic of South Africa is *Official Railway Tariff Book, No. 29*, Rhodesia Railways.

TABLE 7. *Estimated Profit or Loss of Principal Traffics on Rhodesia Railways, 150 Mile Equal Point*

(Tonnage in short tons)

(July 1, 1962–June 30, 1963)

Principal Categories of Traffic	Cost per Ton^a (£)	Cost per Ton^b					Revenue per Ton^c (£)	Profit or Loss per Ton (£)	PROFIT or LOSS (on total tonnage carried of each traffic) (£)	Product Origin
		Terminal	+	Line Haul	=	Total (£)				
General Goods^d	2.59	.71	+	1.88	=	2.59	3.10	+ .51	2,494,294.74	Zambia and Rhodesia
(Tobacco)	1.11	.71	+	.81	=	1.52	2.09	+ .57	(97,914.60)	Mostly Rhodesia
Maize and maize meal	1.14	.71	+	.83	=	1.54	0.84	— .70	(455,585.20)	Mostly Rhodesia
Asbestos	1.47	.71	+	1.01	=	1.72	1.55	— .17	23,651.76	Rhodesia
Chrome Ore	2.29	.71	+	1.21	=	1.92	0.69	—1.23	483,750.39	Rhodesia
Copper^e										
ZAMBIA										
Full Rate										
Beira	8.24	.71	+	5.98	=	6.69	13.82	+7.13	1,444,352.62	Zambia
Lourenço-Marques	7.34	.71	+	5.33	=	6.04	12.33	+6.29	1,706,716.02	
Discount Rate										
Beira	8.24	.71	+	5.98	=	6.69	9.05	+2.36	103,132.00	
Lourenço-Marques	7.34	.71	+	5.33	=	6.04	8.09	+2.05	103,375.35	
To South African Republic	8.22	.71	+	5.97	=	6.68	15.36	+8.68	205,559.76	
CONGO										
Beira (first 70,000 tons)	8.30	.71	+	6.03	=	6.74	14.04	+7.30	511,000.00	Congo
Beira (excess of 70,000 tons)	8.30	.71	+	6.03	=	6.74	11.90	+5.16	103,585.40	
To South African Republic	8.29	.71	+	6.02	=	6.73	15.18	+8.45	31,391.75	
LOCAL RAILINGS										
Zinc and Lead	7.44	.71	+	5.40	=	6.11	6.42	+ .31	24,777.37	Zambia
Other Minerals	n.a.	n.a.		n.a.			0.67	n.a.	n.a.	n.a.
Livestock	1.05	.71	+	.76	=	1.47	1.47	0.00	0.00	Mostly Rhodesia
Coal and Coke	3.01	.71	+	2.19	=	2.90	1.34	—1.56	3,876,599.72	Rhodesia

For footnotes see Table 6.

TABLE 8. *Estimated Profit or Loss of Principal Traffics on Rhodesia Railways, 100 Mile Equal Point*

(Tonnage in short tons)

(July 1, 1962–June 30, 1963)

Principal Categories of Traffic	Cost per Ton[a] (£)	Cost per Ton[b] Terminal	+ Line Haul	= Total (£)	Revenue per Ton[c] (£)	Profit or Loss per Ton (£)	PROFIT or LOSS (on total tonnage carried of each traffic) (£)	Product Origin
General Goods[d]	2.59	.53	+ 2.06	= 2.59	3.10	+ .51	2,494,294.74	Zambia and Rhodesia
(Tobacco)	1.11	.53	+ .86	= 1.39	2.09	+ .70	(120,246.00)	Mostly Rhodesia
(Maize and maize meal)							(390,501.60)	Mostly Rhodesia
Asbestos	1.14	.53	+ .91	= 1.44	0.84	− .60	12,521.52	Rhodesia
Chrome Ore	1.47	.53	+ 1.11	= 1.64	1.55	− .09	460,152.81	Rhodesia
Copper[e]	2.29	.53	+ 1.33	= 1.86	0.69	− 1.17		
ZAMBIA								
Full Rate								
Beira	8.24	.53	+ 6.56	= 7.09	13.82	+ 6.73	1,363,323.02	
Lourenço-Marques	7.34	.53	+ 5.84	= 6.37	12.33	+ 5.96	1,617,174.48	Zambia
Discount Rate								
Beira	8.24	.53	+ 6.56	= 7.09	9.05	+ 1.96	85,652.00	
Lourenço-Marques	7.34	.53	+ 5.84	= 6.37	8.09	+ 1.72	86,734.44	
To South African Republic	8.22	.53	+ 6.55	= 7.08	15.36	+ 8.28	196,086.96	
CONGO								
Beira (first 70,000 tons)	8.30	.53	+ 6.61	= 7.14	14.04	+ 6.90	483,000.00	Congo
Beira (excess of 70,000 tons)	8.30	.53	+ 6.61	= 7.14	11.90	+ 4.76	95,509.40	
To South African Republic	8.29	.53	+ 6.60	= 7.13	15.18	+ 8.05	29,905.75	
LOCAL RAILINGS	n.a.					n.a.		
Zinc and Lead	7.44	.53	+ 5.92	= 6.45	6.42	− .03	2,397.81	Zambia
Other Minerals	n.a.		n.a.		0.67	n.a.	n.a.	n.a.
Livestock	1.05	.53	+ .83	= 1.36	1.47	+ .11	23,364.66	Mostly Rhodesia
Coal and Coke	3.01	.53	+ 2.40	= 2.93	1.34	− 1.59	3,441,534.33	Rhodesia

For footnotes see Table 6.

51

and line-haul—must be separated. This was done by assuming 100 miles, 150 miles, and 200 miles as the distances at which terminal cost per ton equaled line-haul charges.[17] While still crude estimates, the resulting figures at least take some account of the cost differences of short and long hauls.

Regardless of which terminal cost is used, however, on a fully distributed cost basis, Zambian traffic provides large "excess profits" and Rhodesian traffic large "losses." The general goods category would have to consist entirely of high-valued Rhodesian traffic in order to change the essential truth of the case, and there is no evidence that this is so.[18] Moreover, since Zambian traffic is largely bulk traffic, the use of average costs for terminal and line-haul instead of specific costs for each commodity understates the degree to which "excess profits" are made on Zambian traffic and also understates the "losses" on Rhodesian traffic.

It is a mistake to assume that the low rate on Wankie (Rhodesian) coal which is consumed by Zambian and Congolese copper producers "makes up" for any overcharge on copper. Table 7, for example, shows that coal revenues failed to meet fully distributed costs by nearly £3.4 million and therefore seems to support the contention. Closer examination, however, reveals that of the total of 2,164,000 tons of coal moved, only about 700,000 tons were supplied to Zambian copper producers, who are the only large users of coal in Zambia. Using the cost estimates of Table 7 and looking only at Zambia, the low coal rate fails to "make up" the overcharge on copper by about £2,471,000. Were more pre-

[17] Calculations based on a one month's sample of traffic by the Harragin Commission give an average value of terminal costs at about £.67 per ton. Farquharson estimates an average figure of £.70 per ton, both of which indicate that the 150 mile point (Table 7) may be more nearly accurate. The only African rail studies directed specifically to this point suggest 186 miles (BCK) and 200 miles (Nigeria). See the Harragin Report and Farquharson previously cited. Definitional problems abound, however, and precision in absolute amounts is not claimed.

[18] The two Rhodesian commodities which could be pulled out of general goods, tobacco and maize, exert in combination a downward pressure on the profit in this category, but this fact is misleading. The proportion of imported manufactured goods going to Zambia and Rhodesia respectively would determine whether this category supports or mitigates the case, but it could not change the direction of income transfer.

cise estimates made of the relative benefit to Rhodesia and Zambia resulting from the low coal rate, it is likely that Rhodesia, in whose economy the mines are included, would be shown to be the chief beneficiary of the low rate. As it is, and with the understanding that the coal rate covers slightly more than marginal hauling costs,[19] both countries would seem to benefit by the coal rate. An inquiry into costs of coal production at Wankie, including wage policy, and alternative supply possibilities for coal would be necessary in order to trace through the relative benefits to each country.

Although comparable figures are not available, the composition of transit versus local traffic suggests that Angola, like Rhodesia, enjoys lower rail rates on its products as a result of Zambian and Congolese traffic. With low-rated manganese "tied" to high-rated copper shipments, it is possible that the Congo has successfully overcome this problem and may, in fact, contribute very little to Angola.

It is important to be clear about what is implied by these income transfers and what is not. Returning to the basic philosophy of value-of-service pricing, we must remember that no traffic is carried at less than its marginal cost. The issue is not one of traffic subsidy in an economic sense. The issue is that the *level* of these marginal costs is low because of the size of the railway plant which can be supported by the value-of-service rates and that the support comes from one national economy while the benefit goes to another.

A Rail Rate Policy for South Central Africa

It was suggested earlier that general economic considerations call for abandoning the agreements and conventions which restrict traffic to particular ports and railways and prohibit rate competition by the railways serving the area. The problems created by the present rate philosophy suggest that abandonment of the agreements and conventions is also necessary to correct the

[19] Harragin Commission Report, *op. cit.*, p. 45.

faults of the present rating structure. The encouragement of rate competition among the railways will have its greatest impact on the currently high-rated commodities—imports and copper—and will tend to reduce these rates on average. As suggested earlier, differentiation of transport service will probably result in a range of rates for each commodity to choose from, depending on the relative benefits of speed and costs to each. The Benguela, with faster service to and from Europe and America, can charge for this service advantage. In general, however, the charges on high-rated commodities will move downward toward the cost of carrying them. This movement is, of course, what frightens the railways. Such reductions could spell the end of their ability to support themselves at present levels of investment and traffic. This would have repercussions on general rate levels, possible governmental subsidies for the railways, and complications on their international debt, particularly on that borne by Rhodesia Railways. These repercussions are not inevitable. If the railways continue to be reasonably efficient and take the future as well as the present into their pricing and service decisions, it is just as likely that all three can continue to be profitable enterprises.

Even if the railways cannot remain self-supporting, the case for free rail competition is still persuasive. For any of the governments involved, it is preferable that subsidies to a railway, or to any other productive activity, be faced consciously as a part of planned economic development rather than automatically through an earmarked tax whose incidence and use is unrelated to general economic policy goals. Further, present levels of rail investment may not be correct and, within limits, rail competition can be used as one tool in determining proper rail size. Shrinkage of the rail plant is an alternative to government subsidy and may be indicated in the Rhodesia Railways case.

The practical difficulties of promoting a policy of rail rate competition are severe. Each railway is at present better off under the present rate structure than it would be under competitive conditions. How then can rail competition be fostered? Those who have most to gain—Congo and Zambia—must take the lead in encouraging competition for their trade. Fortunately, each is in control of a rail line, or part of one, which can be used for this purpose. The copper companies are located in these same two countries. Zambian governmental policy should work to free the copper producers from restrictions on traffic routing and at the same time work for lower Rhodesia Railways rates for both its own and Congolese copper. The Congo should also use its own route to Matadi for the same sort of bargaining. The combined efforts may convince Rhodesia Railways and the Benguela Railway that the time of excessively high markups on copper is ending. The Benguela, with restrictions lifted, can recoup much of its loss in the short run through active promotion of its unused capacity on inbound shipments to Zambia. The construction of the Cubal Variant would allow it to compete for a larger share of the copper exports but possibly not at the present rate level.

The overall effect of encouraging rail competition, it must be emphasized, is not to overthrow the value-of-service pricing philosophy but to correct its excesses. Profit maximization would be encouraged as a policy on all three railways because, through the pursuit of such a policy under competitive conditions, both technical efficiency and correct investment (and disinvestment) decisions would be encouraged.[20]

[20] For a detailed examination of value-of-service pricing under competitive conditions, see Wilson, *op. cit.*, Chap. 5.

CHAPTER V

New Rail Investments

A<small>N UNFORTUNATE CONSEQUENCE</small> of the present political pattern of South Central Africa, with white minority governments in some countries and African governments in others, is the tendency of nationalistic politics to overshadow long-run economic patterns. Present legal restrictions on traffic and rate policies reinforce the efforts of certain African governments, notably that of Zambia, to consider seriously the very expensive course of a new rail link from Zambia to Dar es Salaam.

While the preceding sections have argued that such a link is economically not justifiable,[1] the political virtues from a Zambian standpoint of a rail link to the sea through a "friendly" country are so strong that the issue must be examined further.

Tan-Zam Rail Link

Figure 3 shows the general alignment of the proposed rail link, which is estimated to cost upwards of £60 million. Also shown is the existing road, not all-weather at present, which more or less parallels the proposed railway. A brief summary of the economic arguments against the line follows:

1. Present and projected trade between the two countries is not sufficient to make the line either economically or financially

[1] As have two survey missions from the World Bank, the UN Economic Commission for Africa report previously cited, and an earlier consultant's report done for the United Kingdom Colonial Office—*Report on Central African Rail Link Development Survey*, 2 vols. (London, 1952).

FIGURE 3. *Proposed Additions to Transport Network*

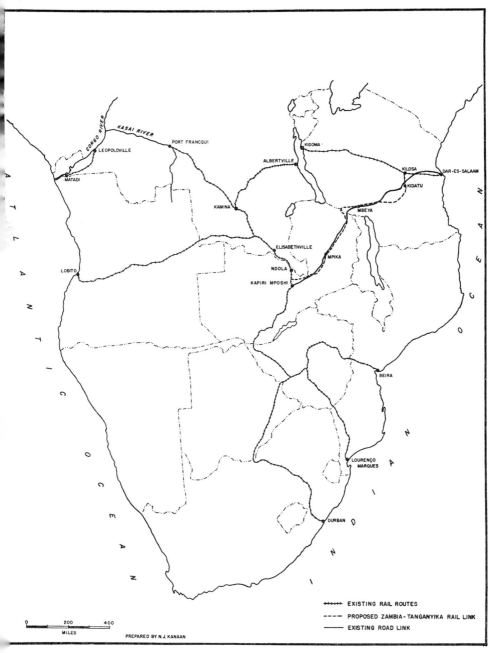

57

attractive. This is emphasized by the high cost characteristics of the proposed link, due in part to terrain and to the gauge problem.

2. Were it to be built, traffic from present rail routes, in particular copper, might be diverted. The financial repercussions of this on present railways would be severe.

3. The port of Dar es Salaam is inadequate to handle much additional traffic, and substantial investment would be needed (not included in the rail link investment estimate) to make the rail link usable.

Further, it is argued that improvements in the present road, estimated by the World Bank at £11 million, could more than handle the projected trade between the two countries and also serve as a generator of economic development in northeast Zambia and southwest Tanganyika.

The economics of the rail link are clearly not persuasive. What remains are the political issues which are often clothed in economic dress[2] and the undoubted fact that in this part of Africa, economic development still means railways. The political appeal of roads has not yet achieved the same status.

No argument couched in economic terms has so far moved the Zambian government to abandon its political goal of freeing itself from dependence on rail routes which run through countries at present dominated by white minority governments. Perhaps it is too much to expect any nation to remain vulnerable in such a fashion if any way can be found, however expensive, to avoid it.

An Alternative to the Rail Link

One alternative which should be seriously considered is the possibility that the railways in South Central Africa might be "Pan-Africanized," not in the sense of replacing European staff with Africans but in the much more fundamental sense of remov-

[2] For example, the recent talk of an economic common market tying together Zambia, Tanzania, Uganda, Kenya, Somalia, and Ethiopia reported in *The Central African Mail*, Feb. 19, 1965, p. 2. Zambian participation in this market could be done by road as well as by rail.

ing them from nationalist politics. Consonant with the freeing of each country from past agreements and conventions, allowing rail competition, and conforming to the terms of the United Nations draft convention on landlocked countries is the notion that the use of the railways is a right. The current placement of the routes is a historical accident of little intrinsic moment to present-day Africa. If Africa develops toward greater regional economic integration, the question of who originally invested what where will have even less relevance for the future.

What is immensely relevant is that capital should be used productively. Duplicating rail lines for short-run political gain is not an example of the productive use of capital. Working toward a system whereby existing resources can be utilized productively would be.

"Pan-Africanization" of the railways involves the following substantive points: (1) recognition that any country may utilize the rail connections physically available to it on the same terms as any other country; (2) no restrictions or quotas on amounts to be shipped by any route or through any port except commercial agreements between shippers and railways; (3) individual railways to be managed as business enterprises with rate and service policies based on profit motives.

These policies could be put into effect through international agreement directly or through some African body such as the UN Economic Commission for Africa. They need not interfere with the present ownership of the railways concerned nor with the inherent profitability of any railway. The rail competition implied would, of course, change present profit patterns.

It may be argued that, except for the Congo and Zambia, none of the other countries—Angola, Mozambique, or Rhodesia—would agree to such policies. It is clear that whatever political advantage these countries enjoy by virtue of their railways and ports would be lost. However, they have really no alternative, because if the Tan-Zam rail link is built, it would strip them of these political advantages *and*, of greater concern, would result in their forever losing the rail traffic from Zambia and possibly much of that from the Congo.

Investment Policy under "Pan-Africanization." Among the many "but what ifs" which can be raised against this suggestion is the issue of investment policy under "Pan-Africanization." Probably cases would arise in which one or more countries disagree with a particular railway regarding the adequacy of investment in line or rolling stock. It might be that both the Congo and Zambia would feel that the Benguela should construct the Cubal Variant, thereby assuring an additional one million tons of capacity each way to the copper mines. The Benguela, on the other hand, viewing its reduced profits in a competitive situation, might demur on the grounds that the capital charges could not be met out of profits. The measure of the Congolese and Zambian interests in the new capacity could in this case be taken by their willingness to cooperate in the financing of the construction.

In another case, one country, say Mozambique, might plan to build a new railway unconnected to the international system and to raise all rail rates to finance the construction. By doing so, they would make their own international route less competitive. At present they may raise their rates without any such constraint.

Rate Policy under "Pan-Africanization." Assuming a value-of-service rate system modified by competition, the "Pan-Africanization" policy should not create difficulties of rate policy. It may be, of course, that some countries will decide to subsidize an industry such as agriculture. Under "Pan-Africanization" the country could not force any railway to lower its rates on any commodity, but it could either pay a part of the rate to the railway or to the producer directly if it chose. Countries could protect themselves, moreover, from excessive rates not only by competitive forces if the railway is in another country but also by their right to tax away excess profits if the railway is within their own borders.

The most important thing to keep in mind in evaluating the "Pan-Africanization" concept is that no change in ownership or management is contemplated. The only thing which changes is the ability of any nation to use for political motives the railway and port which it happens to possess. As an alternative to the costly Tan-Zam link, "Pan-Africanization" is worthy of serious attention.

CHAPTER VI

Transport Regionalism in Africa

AFRICA HAS MANY internal political boundaries which do not coincide with economic regions. The past history of how these boundaries were formed is of little present concern, but the situation in South Central Africa illustrates that the transport patterns which developed as a result of these boundaries may have great influence on future transport investments.

An early pioneer in sociological research, W. I. Thomas, stated "if men define situations as real, they are real in their consequences." Thus if the copper "cannot" go out one way, it will have to go out another. Where it can be shown that the "cannots" are man-made and the costs of indulging the consequences are great, then it is useful to seek a new definition of the situation.

While many of the leaders of the new nations in Africa are riding nationalist tigers, they are aware of the necessity for economic cooperation with their neighbors. There are problems in reconciling the national interests of Uganda, Tanzania, and Kenya, but the rewards of creating a larger economic unit are great, and hence work on East African cooperation continues.

Transport systems are the worst violators of national boundaries and the most sensitive to discrepancies between political and economic boundaries. The complex transport story of copper in South Central Africa points up this fact and calls special attention to the future consequences of past errors. The rail link from Zambia to Tanganyika is one of several transport investments either built or proposed in Africa which can find no justification except in "unreal" definitions. Not all of this unreality is found on the borders between "black" Africa and "white" Africa; some is found on the borders of former French Africa and former English Africa.

Of course, political differences among nations have a logic of their own, and men can bear high costs if their principles are secure. The nations of Europe are evidence of that. Europe also provides evidence of the strength of regional economic logic, as integration of national economies is taking place at last.

The barriers to regional economic cooperation are already formidable in Africa, but the need is far greater than it was in Europe. Most of the new nations literally cannot afford the luxury of inefficient transport connections to the outside world. When the choice is between utilizing a system already in place or building a new one, the issue is even more clearly drawn.

Cooperative regional arrangements in transport are among the easiest international arrangements to work out. Usually the benefits accruing to all parties are immediately apparent and their value known. Moreover, the benefits are not gained by one party as a result of a loss by another party. The costs of regional cooperation in transport are usually low. The arrangements most often involve making new international agreements or reworking old agreements. Often the psychic costs of such negotiation may be high, but the economic costs are low.

The administrative machinery used in operating regional arrangements may, as was the case in East Africa, come to be used for other complementary services. Considerable savings of extremely scarce administrative personnel can result from regional arrangements, even if actual operation continues to be national or private. The work involved in the rather mundane details of transport agreements provides the necessary foundation for broader economic cooperation.

Utilizing existing transport facilities and planning new transport investments in Africa are tasks for which nationalist definitions are tragically wrong. Money spent on unneeded transport capacity is money unspent on much needed educational capacity. Inefficient routing and rate structures add unnecessarily to the costs of African firms competing in world markets and slow the rate of industrial growth.

The amount of short-term advantage one nation in Africa can take over another because of the present transport situation is small compared to the long-run advantage to all Africa of having an efficient transport system based on the economic facts of the continent. The skills and trust which could be acquired in planning such a system cooperatively would surely not go unused in the larger process of uniting Africa.

Appendixes

TRIPARTITE AGREEMENT between the COMPAN-
HIA DO CAMINHO DE FERRO DE BENGUELA, the
COMPAGNIE DU CHEMIN DE FER DU BAS-CONGO
AU KATANGA and the RHODESIA RAILWAYS, relating
to the passage of goods traffic between Lobito and the
Rhodesia Railways.

WHEREAS it is expedient for an agreement to be concluded between the administration of the COMPANHIA
DO CAMINHO DE FERRO DE BENGUELA, the COM-
PAGNIE DU CHEMIN DE FER DU BAS-CONGO AU
KATANGA and the RHODESIA RAILWAYS for the interchange of traffic, rating, allocation of revenue, and other
relevant matters concerning the passage of through goods
traffic between Lobito and the Rhodesia Railways.

NOW therefore this instrument serves to record that the
parties have agreed as follows:

Definitions.

"R.R." shall mean the Administration of the Rhodesia
Railways.

"C.F.B." shall mean the Companhia do Caminho de
Ferro de Benguela.

"B.C.K." shall mean the lines operated by the Compagnie du Chemin de Fer du Bas-Congo au Katanga.

"NORTHERN RAILWAYS" shall mean the C.F.B. and
the B.C.K.

"CONGO BORDER" shall mean the point at which the
Railway line from Ndola in Northern Rhodesia to Sakania
in the Belgian Congo crosses the border between Northern
Rhodesia and the Belgian Congo.

"S.A.R." shall mean the South African Railways and
Harbours.

"T.Z.R." shall mean the Trans-Zambezia Railway Company, Limited, and the Nyasaland Railways, Limited.

"C.F.M.(B)" shall mean the Caminho de Ferro da Beira.

"C.F.M." shall mean the Portos e Caminhos de Ferro
da Provincia de Mocambique.

"THROUGH TRAFFIC" shall mean traffic from Lobito
on the C.F.B. to points on the lines owned by the R.R. south
of Congo Border and vice versa and shall further mean

traffic conveyed from or to Lobito over the lines of the C.F.B. and the B.C.K. and the R.R. in transit to or from other Railways.

Article 1.
Special
Facilities.

It is agreed between the parties that traffic between Lobito and the R.R. shall be afforded special facilities as provided in this Agreement in addition to such other general arrangements set out in the Agreement between the B.C.K. and the R.R. as may be applicable.

Article 2.
C.F.B. to
Accept
Conditions.

The C.F.B. accept the conditions of the Working Agreement between the R.R. and the B.C.K. which affect any of the aspects of the through traffic between Lobito and places south of Congo Border.

Article 3.
Acceptance
of Traffic.

The contracting Administrations agree that they will accept for transport in both directions goods of any description subject to the tonnage limitation specified in Article 5 and as far as may be practicable to the general conditions of carriage laid down in the Official Tariff Books of the conveying Administrations.

Article 4.
Through
Traffic:
Provision
of Goods
Vehicles.

(i) Except as otherwise may be mutually arranged the contracting Administrations agree—

(a) that the provision of vehicles for the conveyance of through goods traffic to and from Lobito will not devolve upon the R.R., and

(b) that they will not utilise the vehicles of the other for local traffic, except in the direction of the parent line.

(ii) If at any time the balance in interchange is regarded by any Administration as excessive, the defaulting Administration shall, on representations to it, take such steps as may be necessary to reduce the adverse balance.

Article 5.
Volume of
Traffic.

The contracting Administrations agree that there shall be no limitation on the tonnage of goods to be conveyed to places south of Congo Border from Lobito for the first twelve months of operation of this Agreement, but that the matter will be reviewed at the end of the first twelve months and every twelve months thereafter. The tonnage of goods to be conveyed from places south of Congo Border to Lobito for shipment shall similarly be unlimited except that in the case of Copper no greater tonnage shall be accepted by the contracting parties for export via Lobito than 10% of the present railings by the Northern Rhodesia Copper Mines to Beira and Lourenço Marques plus 50% of any additional tonnage which would be available for railing to Beira and Lourenço Marques in the future subject to no higher tonnage than 20% of the total tonnage available for export overseas. If any modification in these tonnages is agreed by the appropriate authorities in the Federation, this article shall be suitably amended by an exchange of letters between the parties.

Article 6.
Rates for
Imported
Goods via
Lobito to
Places South
of Congo
Border.

(i)   For traffic consigned to Ndola and to Bwana Mkubwa and places on the Roan Antelope, Nchanga, Bancroft and Mufulira branch lines, the rates from Lobito, with the exception of coal, shall be those applicable from time to time from Beira to the destination station.

(ii)   For traffic consigned to places on the R.R. beyond Ndola in the direction of Livingstone, the rates from Lobito shall be the sum of the rates from Beira to Ndola and the distribution rates compiled in terms of the Official R.R. Tariff Book from Ndola to destination on the R.R. The actual throughout rates chargeable from time to time will be notified by the R.R. to the B.C.K. for transmission to the C.F.B.

(iii)   In the case of goods consigned from Lobito to Ndola, Nkana, Broken Hill, Lusaka and such other points as the R.R. may from time to time determine and subsequently distributed from any of these points to other places on the R.R., the R.R. agree to apply the distribution rates operative according to the regulations contained in the Official Tariff Book of the R.R.

(iv)   Subarticles (ii) and (iii) are subject to review by the R.R. at any time after consultation with the other parties if, in the opinion of the R.R., such action is necessary or desirable in terms of any agreements already in existence between the R.R. or the Federal or other Government and other parties.

(v)   In the event of traffic being consigned from Lobito to places on the S.A.R., C.F.M., the C.F.M.(B) or the T.Z.R., the normal rates applicable to such traffic from time to time over the C.F.B. and B.C.K. to Congo Border, plus the normal rates applicable from Congo Border to destination according to the rating arrangements applicable between the R.R. and the Administrations concerned shall be maintained.

Article 7.
Rates for
Goods to
Lobito from
Places South
of Congo
Border.

(i)   For general goods and mineral traffic other than copper, the rates shall be the normal rates applicable according to the R.R. Official Tariff Books from the point of despatch to Congo Border plus the normal rates applicable to such traffic over the B.C.K. and the C.F.B.

(ii)   For copper from the Northern Rhodesia Copper Mines to Lobito, throughout rates, which will not be less than the rates applicable from the Northern Rhodesia Copper Mines to Beira and Lourenço Marques shall be charged. The actual rates charged by each Administration from time to time shall be advised to the other.

Article 8.
Division of
Receipts.

The division of receipts for through goods traffic from Lobito to places south of Congo Border and vice versa shall be as follows—

(i)   In respect of traffic conveyed from Lobito to places on the R.R. south of Congo Border, the R.R. shall receive its full local rate for the journey from Congo Border to destination plus the amounts stated in Article 10 where applicable and the Northern Railways shall receive the balance.

(ii)   In respect of traffic conveyed from Lobito to places on the S.A.R., the C.F.M., C.F.M.(B) or the T.Z.R., the R.R. and the contiguous Administrations concerned shall receive the rates normally applicable from Congo Border to destination and the Northern Railways shall receive their rates.

(iii)   In respect of traffic consigned from places on the R.R. south of Congo Border to Lobito for shipment, excluding copper, each Administration shall receive its own rate.

(iv)   In respect of Copper consigned from the Northern Rhodesia Copper Mines to Lobito for shipment and charged at agreed through rates, the Northern Railways shall receive on all copper consigned from the Copperbelt area 92% of the through rate from Ndola to Lobito applicable from time to time and the R.R. shall receive the balance.

(v)   In respect of traffic consigned via Congo Border from places on the S.A.R., C.F.M., C.F.M.(B) and T.Z.R. to Lobito for shipment, the R.R. and the contiguous Administrations concerned shall receive the rates normally applicable from the sending station to Congo Border and the Northern Railways shall receive their rates.

Article 9.
Entry of
Through
Goods
Traffic.

Charges entries which shall contain the English language, weights and measures and the currency of the Federation of Rhodesia and Nyasaland for through goods traffic, will be passed as follows—

(i)   In respect of traffic from Lobito to places on the R.R. only, the C.F.B. shall pass an invoice to the destination station for the total charges which shall be entered either prepaid or for collection at the destination.

(ii) In respect of traffic from Lobito to places on the C.F.M.(B), C.F.M., S.A.R. and T.Z.R., the C.F.B. shall pass an invoice to Ndola for the destination but such invoice shall only contain the charges for the journey to Congo Border which shall be prepaid at Lobito. The charges from Congo Border to the destination station shall be raised locally by the R.R.

(iii) In respect of traffic, excluding copper, consigned from places on the R.R. south of Congo Border to Lobito for shipment the R.R. shall pass an invoice to Ndola for Lobito, such invoice accounting for the charges from the sending station to Congo Border only, the charges so entered being prepaid at the sending station.

(iv) In respect of copper consigned from the Northern Rhodesia Copper Mines to Lobito for shipment the R.R. sending station shall pass an invoice for the total agreed throughout rate to Lobito, the total charges being prepaid.

Article 10. Terminal and Other Payments to the R.R. By the Northern Railways.

(i) It is agreed that the Northern Railways will pay to the R.R. the amount of 5/- per ton in respect of all import traffic passing via Lobito to points on the R.R. within 60 miles of Congo Border in respect of the terminal costs incurred by the R.R.

(ii) The Northern Railways shall also pay to the R.R. on all import traffic classified at Tariffs 1 to 10 plus or less percentages via Lobito to points south of Congo Border on the R.R., an amount per ton assessed from time to time as being the average cost per ton to the R.R. of the quotation of distribution rates instead of local rates for traffic reforwarded from the distribution centres stated in Article 6 (iii). For the first twelve months the additional amount payable shall be 2/6 per ton and such records shall be maintained by the R.R. as will enable a review of this charge to be undertaken at the end of the first and every subsequent twelve months period.

Article 11. Interpretation in Terms of Agreement.

All matters not specifically provided for in this Agreement and all things necessary to promote efficient cooperation shall be arranged from time to time by conference or correspondence between the R.R., the B.C.K. and the C.F.B. All questions arising between these Administrations in respect of the application of this Agreement or the interpretation of the terms thereof shall form the subject of free consultations between the General Managers of the C.F.B., the B.C.K. and the R.R. Any dispute which may arise out of the interpretation or application of this Agreement and which cannot be resolved by consultation between the General Managers of the Contracting Administrations shall be submitted to arbitration. The B.C.K. and the C.F.B. shall jointly appoint one arbitrator, and the R.R. shall appoint one arbitrator. These arbitrators, before proceeding to consider the question, shall agree upon and appoint a third, the award of the majority to be final and binding.

Article 12.
Period of
Operation of
Agreement.

This Agreement shall be deemed to have come into operation as from the 1st January, 1957. It shall be operative for a period of four years from this date, but it shall be reviewed at the end of the first year to determine whether the technical and financial problems of the Administrations concerned necessitate any amendments within its framework. Any portion of the Agreement, however, may be modified at any time with the consent of the parties.

IN WITNESS WHEREOF, we have hereunder placed our hand to duplicate originals hereof in the presence of the under-mentioned witnesses:

on the 7th November, 1956.   Signed by HENRY BREEDON EVERARD in his capacity as GENERAL MANAGER of the RHODESIA RAILWAYS; at BULAWAYO, and as such representing the RHODESIA RAILWAYS ADMINISTRATION.

AS WITNESSES:

. . . .

. . . .

on the 7th November, 1956.   Signed by LEONARD LOUIS GHYSE-
LINCK in his capacity as ACTING GEN-
ERAL MANAGER of the COMPAGNIE
DU CHEMIN DE FER DU BAS-CONGO
AU KATANGA at ELISABETHVILLE,
and as such representing the COMPAGNIE
DU CHEMIN DE FER DU BAS-CONGO
AU KATANGA.

AS WITNESSES:

. . . .

. . . .

on the 7th November, 1956.   Signed by ROBERT JAMES WALKER in
his capacity as EXECUTIVE DIRECTOR
of the COMPANHIA DO CAMINHO DE
FERRO DE BENGUELA at LISBON, and
as such representing the COMPANHIA DO
CAMINHO DE FERRO DE BENGUELA.

AS WITNESSES:

. . . .

. . . .

APPENDIX B

CONVENTION BETWEEN THE GOVERNMENT OF THE
UNITED KINGDOM OF GREAT BRITAIN AND NORTHERN
IRELAND ON THEIR OWN BEHALF AND ON BEHALF
OF THE GOVERNMENT OF SOUTHERN RHODESIA
AND THE GOVERNMENT OF THE REPUBLIC OF PORTUGAL
RELATIVE TO THE PORT OF BEIRA AND CONNECTED RAILWAYS

Lisbon, 17th June, 1950

The Government of the United Kingdom of Great Britain and Northern Ireland (hereinafter called the Government of the United Kingdom) on their own behalf and on behalf of the Government of Southern Rhodesia and the Government of the Republic of Portugal (hereinafter called the Portuguese Government);

Having regard to the situation created by the nationalisation of the Rhodesia Railways and its effect on the operation of the Beira Railway;

Having regard to the acquisition of the Beira Works Limited and the purchase of the Beira Railway Company's assets by the Portuguese Government;

Having regard to the importance of the Port of Beira and its railway communications with the interior of Africa as an outlet for the resources of the territories of Southern Rhodesia, Northern Rhodesia and Nyasaland, and to the progressive contribution which they can make to the development of Mozambique;

Considering that the maintenance of adequate facilities at the Port of Beira and over the Beira Railway is and will continue to be of vital interest to the territories in question;

Desiring to cooperate fully with a view to the development of the resources of Mozambique on the one hand and of Southern Rhodesia, Northern Rhodesia and Nyasaland on the other in conformity with the principles set out in the Convention for European Economic Cooperation, and thereby to contribute, in so far as each party is able, to the restoration of world prosperity and the development of the Central African territories for the benefit of the inhabitants;

Considering the necessity of carrying out works and other improvements in connexion with the Port of Beira and the Beira Railway to achieve the objects mentioned above and the advantage of arriving at a mutual understanding which will make such improvements economically realisable;

74

Have resolved to enter into a Convention for that purpose and have appointed as their representatives to that end, that is to say:

The Government of the United Kingdom—

Sir Nigel Bruce Ronald, K.C.M.G., C.V.O., His Britannic Majesty's Ambassador Extraordinary and Plenipotentiary at Lisbon;

The Government of Southern Rhodesia—

The Right Honourable Sir Godfrey Martin Huggins, P.C., C.H., K.C.M.G., Prime Minister of Southern Rhodesia;

The Portuguese Government—

His Excellency Doctor José Caeiro da Matta, Minister of Foreign Affairs;

who, having communicated their respective powers, found in good and due form, have agreed as follows:

ARTICLE I

(a) The Contracting Governments, recognising the substantial investment involved in the obligation to expand the Port of Beira and the Beira Railway assumed by the Portuguese Government under this Convention, adopt as an objective of their common policy that the Port and the Railway should be used to their full working capacity.

(b) To that end if at any time during the currency of the present Convention—

(i) the volume of traffic handled by the Port of Beira or the Beira Railway over any period of six consecutive months falls substantially below the full working capacity of the said port or railway in their present state or at any stage of their progressive expansion in accordance with the provisions of paragraph (a) of Article III, or

(ii) it is established that the use of the Port of Beira or the Beira Railway up to such full working capacity is being prevented or is likely to be prevented by any change in circumstances affecting such use outside the control of the Contracting Governments or not expressly contemplated in the present Convention,

then the Contracting Governments shall, upon the request of either of them consult together with a view to taking such reasonable steps in furtherance of the objective referred to in paragraph (a) of this Article as may be considered necessary and consistent with the efficient and economic employment of the transport resources available to the territories to which the present Convention applies.

(c) The Administrations concerned shall periodically consult together with a view to fixing the full working capacity of the Port of Beira and the Beira Railway for the purpose of this Article.

ARTICLE II

(a) The Government of the United Kingdom in respect of Northern Rhodesia and Nyasaland and the Government of Southern Rhodesia shall not themselves introduce either directly or indirectly, and shall take all reasonable steps within their power to prevent, any discrimination in the territories to which this Convention applies against traffic for which the Port of Beira, on account of its proximity to sources of consumption or origin, is the natural inlet or outlet, and in particular they undertake—

(i) not to permit any discrimination in railway freight rates and charges against such traffic over lines within the territories to which this Convention applies;

(ii) not to permit alterations of railway freight rates over lines within the territories to which this Convention applies nor to enter into agreements with other countries for alterations of railway freight rates, if such alterations contribute materially to the diversion from the Port of Beira and the Beira Railway of traffic which is within the capacity of that Port and Railway;

(iii) not to permit the railway freight rates over the lines within the territories to which this Convention applies on goods proceeding direct to and from the Port of Beira to exceed the railway freight rates on the same goods proceeding direct to and from other ports, in so far as the direct operating costs are similar and distances covered the same;

(iv) (1) to continue to accord the railway rates preferences in favour of the Port of Beira over ports in the Union of South Africa at a level not lower than those set out in the schedule to this Convention, subject to the provisions of section (2) of this sub-paragraph;

(2) if a diminution in such rates preferences should arise from an increase by the Beira Railway of the freight rates over its lines, the possibility of restoring such preferences shall be the subject of consultations between the Railway Administrations concerned. If they are unable to agree on the measures to be taken to adjust the matter to their mutual satisfaction, it shall be referred by them to the Contracting Governments in order that they may consult together in accordance with the previsions of paragraph (b) of Article I;

(v) to maintain the Rhodesia Railways in a state of efficiency adequate to the requirements of the traffic proceeding to or from Beira.

(b) It shall be understood that the provisions of this Article shall be dependent on the maintenance of an adequate service in the Port of Beira and on the Beira Railway, and on the dues, rates and other charges levied on traffic passing through the Port of Beira to or from Southern Rhodesia, Northern Rhodesia or Nyasaland not being such as to make that traffic uneconomic.

ARTICLE III

(a) The Portuguese Government undertake to maintain the Port of Beira and the Beira Railway in a state of efficiency adequate to the requirements of the traffic proceeding to or from Southern Rhodesia, Northern Rhodesia and Nyasaland, to which end they will promote the execution of the works and the acquisition of the equipment necessary for the technical and economic development of the Port of Beira and the Beira Railway and in order to expedite the handling of cargoes and clearance of ships and railway traffic. Particulars of these works and this equipment are contained in the letters exchanged between the Administrations of the Mozambique and Beira Railways and the Rhodesia Railways.

(b) After the completion of the works and the acquisition of the equipment mentioned in the letters exchanged under paragraph (a) of this Article, the Portuguese Government undertake to execute such further works of expansion and acquire such additional equipment as may be required to meet the demands of future traffic and may be found justifiable on technical and economic grounds after full consultation between the Contracting Governments.

(c) In addition, the Contracting Governments shall consult together from time to time with respect to the execution of the works and the acquisition of the equipment required for carrying out the provisions of this Article.

ARTICLE IV

(a) The Contracting Governments shall not permit any modification of the railway rates in force in respect of traffic in transit through Beira without prior consultation with the Administrations concerned, which are as follows:

(i) in the case of through traffic to or from the Rhodesia Railways, the Administrations of the Rhodesia Railways and the Beira Railway;

(ii) in the case of through traffic to or from the Trans-Zambesia Railway, the Administrations of the Trans-Zambesia Railway and the Beira Railway;

(iii) in the case of through traffic to or from the Nyasaland Railways, the Administrations of the Nyasaland Railways and the Beira Railway.

(b) The Portuguese Government shall take all reasonable steps to avoid any discrimination in rates and charges over the Beira Railway against traffic to or from Southern Rhodesia, Northern Rhodesia and Nyasaland.

ARTICLE V

During the currency of the present Convention the Portuguese Government will not exercise their rights to levy transit dues on goods imported or exported through the Port of Beira to or from the territories to which this Convention applies.

This concession does not cover any stamp tax which may be payable.

ARTICLE VI

(a) The passage of persons, goods, vehicles, railway carriages and wagons to or from Mozambique or to or from Southern Rhodesia, Northern Rhodesia or Nyasaland shall not be liable in the territories to which this Convention applies to any interference or restriction except those which are required by police, customs, health and statistical regulations.

(b) The regulations mentioned in paragraph (a) of this Article shall be framed to avoid unnecessary delays which might prevent the rapid transit of persons or goods to or from Mozambique, or to or from Southern Rhodesia, Northern Rhodesia or Nyasaland.

(c) Persons, goods, vehicles, railway carriages and wagons in transit through Mozambique to or from Southern Rhodesia, Northern Rhodesia or Nyasaland shall not be subjected in Mozambique to any discrimination based on their nationality, destination, or place of origin.

The same provisions shall apply to persons, goods, vehicles, railway carriages and wagons in transit to or from Mozambique through Southern Rhodesia, Northern Rhodesia or Nyasaland.

(d) A special agreement shall be made to regulate the customs formalities to be carried out by Southern Rhodesian Customs staff in Beira and by Mozambique Customs staff in Umtali, and to provide for reciprocal facilities for the establishment of such staff in those territories. Similar arrangements shall, if necessary, be made in respect of Northern Rhodesian and Nyasaland Customs staff in Mozambique and Mozambique Customs staff in Northern Rhodesia and Nyasaland.

ARTICLE VII

(a) In the interest of Southern Rhodesia, Northern Rhodesia and Nyasaland, the Portuguese Government shall establish in Beira a free zone into which and from which goods proceeding to or from these territories may be imported, stored, processed, manufactured and exported to foreign countries without payment of any charges in respect of import, export or re-export.

(b) The Portuguese Government shall define the area of the free zone and shall draw up and publish in the shortest time possible the legal provisions governing its utilisation.

ARTICLE VIII

(a) Matters concerning the inter-related workings of the railways of the territories to which the present Convention applies shall be the subject of

Working Agreements to be concluded between the respective Railway Administrations with the approval of the Contracting Governments.

(b) The Working Agreements shall contain provisions whereby alterations and additions thereto may be agreed by the said Railway Administrations, provided always that alterations of or additions to the matters of principle, which are to be defined in Notes to be exchanged by the Contracting Governments in ratification of each such Working Agreement, shall require the prior approval of the Contracting Governments.

(c) After such approval these Working Agreements shall be binding on the Contracting Governments.

ARTICLE IX

The Portuguese Government agree to sell to the Rhodesia Railways the section of the line between Umtali and the frontier of Mozambique on conditions to be agreed between the two Governments.

ARTICLE X

(a) The Portuguese Government shall establish in Beira an Advisory Board, the functions of which shall be to consider and advise as to the best means of developing and facilitating the traffic passing through the Port of Beira and on the Beira Railway to or from Southern Rhodesia, Northern Rhodesia and Nyasaland.

(b) The Portuguese Government shall invite, through the Governments of Southern Rhodesia, Northern Rhodesia, and Nyasaland, the agricultural, commercial, industrial and mining organisations in these territories to nominate between them five representatives to the Board.

(c) Representation on the Board shall be given to shipping companies established in Beira.

(d) Copies of the minutes of the meetings of the Board and of its reports shall be sent to the Governments of Mozambique, Southern Rhodesia, Northern Rhodesia and Nyasaland not later than 15 days after each meeting, without prejudice to the right of the Board to submit its reports to the Portuguese Government also.

ARTICLE XI

The Contracting Governments shall as soon as possible initiate negotiations for the conclusion of Trade and Establishment Agreements applicable between Mozambique on the one hand and the territories of Southern Rhodesia, Northern Rhodesia and Nyasaland on the other hand. It is contemplated that such agreements will include provisions prescribing conditions applicable to the citizens of one party to any such agreement residing in the territories of the other party; for facilitating the passage of citizens of one party travelling to or from the territories of the other party; for regulating customs tariffs between territories of the parties and where possible providing for the free interchange of certain classes of goods; and for the reciprocal appointment by the parties of commercial and other representatives.

ARTICLE XII

(a) Upon the request in writing by one Contracting Government to the other any difference or dispute about the interpretation or application of the present Convention shall be referred to two arbitrators, one to be appointed by each Contracting Government within one month after the date of receipt of any such request.

(b) The two arbitrators shall give their decision within four months of the date on which they are appointed. If they cannot agree on a decision regarding the settlement of the difference or dispute within that time-limit, they shall refer the difference or dispute to a third arbitrator appointed by them, who shall himself decide it within four months from the date on which he is appointed. If the two arbitrators are unable to agree on the appointment of the third arbitrator, he shall be appointed by a third Power designated by the Contracting Governments.

(c) The decision of the two arbitrators or the third arbitrator, if appointed, shall be final and binding on the Contracting Governments.

ARTICLE XIII

(a) The territories to which the present Convention applies are Mozambique, Southern Rhodesia, Northern Rhodesia and Nyasaland.

(b) For the purpose of the present Convention—

(i) "The Beira Railway" is the railway formerly operated under a concession from the Portuguese Government by a company named the "Beira Railway Company Limited" and now the property of the Portuguese Government;

(ii) "Rhodesia Railways" shall mean the railways now owned or operated by the Rhodesia Railways, whose Head Office is at Bulawayo, Southern Rhodesia, with the addition of the section of the line between Umtali and the frontier of Mozambique when acquired;

(iii) "Nyasaland Railways" shall mean the railways now owned by Nyasaland Railways Limited, whose Head Office is in London, including its subsidiary, the Central Africa Railway Company.

(iv) "The Trans-Zambesia Railway" shall mean the railway now owned by the Trans-Zambesia Railway Company, whose Head Office is in London.

(c) The provisions of the present Convention shall apply equally to such new lines as may be opened for operation in the territories mentioned in paragraph (a) of this Article after the entry into force of the present Convention.

ARTICLE XIV

(a) This Convention shall be in force for a period of twenty years from the date of its signature. In case neither of the Contracting Governments shall have given notice to the other six months before the date of expiration of this period of their intention to terminate it, it shall remain in force until the expiration of six months from the date on which either of the Contracting Governments shall have denounced it.

(b) After the expiry of the first ten years from the date of the signature of this Convention, either of the Contracting Governments may request a revision of its terms by giving one year's notice to the other Contracting Government.

In witness whereof the representatives of the respective Governments, being duly authorised to that effect, have signed the present Convention and have affixed thereto their seals.

Done at Lisbon in duplicate in English and Portuguese this seventeenth day of June, 1950, both texts being equally authentic.

(L.S.) N. Ronald   (L.S.) José Caeiro de Matta

APPENDIX C

AGREEMENT

between The Government of Southern Rhodesia
and The Government of Northern Rhodesia
relating to the Rhodesia Railways

An Agreement made and entered into by and between
THE GOVERNMENT OF SOUTHERN RHODESIA of
the first part and THE GOVERNMENT OF NORTHERN
RHODESIA of the second part.

Preamble

WHEREAS the Government of Southern Rhodesia and
the Government of Northern Rhodesia desire that the
Rhodesia Railways should continue as a single undertaking
under the joint ownership and control of the said Governments.

IT IS HEREBY AGREED:

Organization

1. The Rhodesia Railways (hereinafter referred to as the
Railways) will continue under the immediate control of a
board of management (hereinafter referred to as the
Board), which will be responsible on behalf of the two
Governments for the performance of the Railways' func-
tions.

2. The Board will consist of a Chairman and six other
members. The Chairman will be appointed by the Higher
Authority referred to in Article 3 of this Agreement. Of
the six other members three will be appointed by the Government of Southern Rhodesia and three by the Government of Northern Rhodesia. Each Government, before
making an appointment to the Board, shall consult with
the other Government and with the Chairman with a view
to securing that the Board is composed of persons with
diverse technical, professional, business or administrative
qualifications.

3. A Higher Authority for Railways, in this Agreement
called the Higher Authority, will be constituted, composed of two Ministers appointed by each of the two Governments, to exercise functions on their behalf in respect

of the Railways. No decision of the Higher Authority will have effect unless it is unanimous.

Legislation

4. Having been informed by the Government of the United Kingdom of their readiness to take appropriate steps with a view to the submission to Her Majesty in Council of a draft Order in Council containing provisions substantially to the same effect as those set out in Appendix I to this Agreement, the two Governments agree that it is expedient that such provision should be made by Order in Council. They also undertake to secure the enactment, by Regulations made in their respective Territories under the powers that will be conferred by the Order in Council, of provisions amending the existing legislation in their Territories regarding the Railways. These amendments will be, in Southern Rhodesia, those contained in the draft at Appendix II to this Agreement amending the Rhodesia Railways Act 1949 and the Rhodesia Railways Loans Guarantee Act 1950 and, in Northern Rhodesia, those contained in the draft at Appendix III to this Agreement amending the Rhodesia Railways Ordinance 1949 and the Rhodesia Railways Loans Guarantee Ordinance 1950. The drafts contained in Appendices I, II and III form integral parts of this Agreement and each Government agrees that it will not amend, without the agreement of the other Government, the provisions of the Order in Council, when made, relating to the Railways, the existing legislation referred to in this Article as amended by the Regulations when they are made or any legislation of the Territories that may in the future, with the agreement of both Governments, be substituted therefor.

Financial Provision

5. The ownership of the Railways and, subject to the provisions of this Agreement, the financial responsibility for them will lie with the two Governments in equal shares.

6. The Government of Northern Rhodesia undertakes to pay the Government of Southern Rhodesia amounts equal to one half of the payments due from the latter to stockholders in respect of

(a) that part amounting to £30 million which was raised for railway purposes and lent to the Railways out of the loan of £32 million raised on the market by the Government of Southern Rhodesia in 1947 at 2½ percent per annum and repayable in 1965-1970; and

(b) that part, amounting to £5 million, which was lent by the Government of Southern Rhodesia to the Railways, out of a loan of £10 million raised on the market by the Government of Southern Rhodesia in 1953 at 4½ percent per annum and repayable in 1987-1992;

in so far as the payments due to the stockholders on the maturing of these loans cannot be met from the sinking funds held by trustees for the redemption of these loans. Unless otherwise agreed between the Governments, such payments shall be made in sufficient time to enable the Government of Southern Rhodesia to redeem the loans at the latest dates. They agree that, before such payment is made in respect of the loan detailed in paragraph (a) of this Article, they will amend section 19 of the Rhodesia Railways Act, 1949, of Southern Rhodesia, and section 13 of the Rhodesia Railways Ordinance, 1949, of Northern Rhodesia, both as amended by the Regulations referred to in Article 4 of this Agreement or any legislation of the Territories that may in the future, with the agreement of both Governments, be substituted therefor so that all benefits and responsibilities of the Government of Southern Rhodesia as detailed therein are thereafter shared equally between them; and that they will similarly share equally the corresponding benefits and responsibilities in respect of the loan detailed in paragraph (b) of this Article.

7. The Government of Southern Rhodesia undertakes to pay to the Government of Northern Rhodesia an amount equal to one half of the payments due from the latter to stockholders in respect of the loan of £7.73 million raised on the market for railway purposes by the Government of Northern Rhodesia in 1951 at 3½ percent per annum and repayable in 1970-1972, in so far as the payments due to the stockholders on the maturing of this loan cannot be met from the sinking fund held by trustees for its redemption. Unless otherwise agreed between the Governments, such payment shall be made in sufficient time to enable the Government of Northern Rhodesia to redeem the loan at the latest date. They agree that, before such payment is made, they will amend section 19A of the Rhodesia Railways Act, 1949, of Southern Rhodesia, and section 13A of the Rhodesia Railways Ordinance, 1949, of Northern Rhodesia, both as amended by the Regulations referred to in Article 4 of this Agreement, or any legislation of the Territories that may in the future, with

the agreement of both Governments, be substituted therefor so that all benefits and responsibilities of the Government of Northern Rhodesia as detailed therein are thereafter shared equally between them.

8. The Government of Southern Rhodesia will become entitled to one half, and the Government of Northern Rhodesia will become entitled to one half, of each and every payment of interest and repayment of capital due from the Railways in respect of the loans listed in Appendix IV to this Agreement, which were made to the Railways by the Federal Government over the years 1955 to 1959.

9. They agree that the payments due from the Railways in respect of the loans originally totalling £5 million made in 1952 by the Economic Co-operation Administration of the Government of the United States of America to the Government of the United Kingdom, re-lent to the Railways through the Governments of Southern and Northern Rhodesia at 2½ percent per annum and repayable in annual instalments ending in the financial year ending on 30th June 1965 will be made by the Railways direct to the Government of the United Kingdom for payment by them to the Government of the United States of America, and the Governments of Southern and Northern Rhodesia undertake that they will each guarantee to the Government of the United Kingdom one half of each and every payment due from the Railways under this Article.

10. They agree that the Railways should assume the obligations of the Federal Government in respect of the loan originally totalling £3,571,428 11s. 5d. in sterling currency made in 1954 by the Foreign Operations Administration of the Government of the United States of America to the Federal Government, re-lent to the Railways by the Federal Government at 4¾ percent per annum and repayable in annual instalments ending in the financial year ending on 30th June 1976 and they undertake that they will each guarantee to the Government of the United States of America one half of each and every payment which will be due from the Railways to that Government in respect of this loan.

11. They will each assume one half of the liabilities of the Federal Government towards the International Bank for Reconstruction and Development in respect of the loan of $19 million made by the Bank to the Federal

Government in 1958 at 5⅝ percent per annum, repayable
in fifteen equal annual instalments of capital and interest
ending in 1976 and re-lent on the same terms by the Federal Government to the Railways. Similarly each and every
payment due from the Railways in respect of this loan will
be made as to one half to the Government of Southern
Rhodesia and as to one half to the Government of Northern Rhodesia.

12. Subject to any agreement that may be reached between them and the Government of the United Kingdom
to the contrary, the Governments of Southern Rhodesia
and Northern Rhodesia will each become liable for one
half of that part of the liabilities of the Federal Government to the Export Credit Guarantees Department of the
Government of the United Kingdom under the United
Kingdom-Federation of Rhodesia and Nyasaland Credit
Agreement 1962, which relates to purchases made or to be
made by the Railways under that Credit Agreement and
in respect of which payment has not been made by the
Railways to the Federal Government. The Railways will
become liable to the Government of Southern Rhodesia
for one half and to the Government of Northern Rhodesia
for one half of the payments due from the Railways in respect of these purchases in terms of the letter from the
Federal Ministry of Transport to the Railways of 1st July
1963 concerning such purchases.

13. The Governments, taking note of the obligations of
the Railways in respect of the following loans to the Railways—

(a) those mentioned in Articles 6 to 12 of this Agreement;

(b) that of £ 2,000,000 made by the Government of
Northern Rhodesia, repayable in full in 1973; and

(c) that of $14 million made by the International
Bank for Reconstruction and Development through the
Government of Northern Rhodesia, repayable by 1972;
recognize and accept the mutual guarantees effectively
created by the provisions of sections 25 and 26 of the Rhodesia Railways Act 1949 of Southern Rhodesia and the
provisions of sections 19 and 20 of the Rhodesia Railways Ordinance 1949 of Northern Rhodesia, both as
amended by the Regulations referred to in Article 4 of this
Agreement.

14. They will each guarantee to the Rhodesia Railways

Pension Funds half of each and every payment due from the railways in respect of the loans listed in Appendix V to this Agreement and will each accept half of the other obligations of the Federal Government in respect of the Railways Pension Funds under the Rhodesia Railways Loans Guarantee Act 1950 of Southern Rhodesia and the Rhodesia Railways Loans Guarantee Ordinance 1950 of Northern Rhodesia.

15. In the event of the Higher Authority agreeing that the Railways should be provided with additional capital from the two Governments or that guarantees should be given by those Governments in respect of loans or credits to be obtained by the Railways from other sources, such additional capital or guarantees will, except as provided in Articles 38 and 39 of this Agreement, be provided or given by the two Governments in equal amounts or in such other proportions as they may agree.

16. In the event of the Railways requiring in any year a contribution from the Governments in terms of section 26 of the Rhodesia Railways Act 1949 of Southern Rhodesia and section 20 of the Rhodesia Railways Ordinance 1949 of Northern Rhodesia, both as amended by the Regulations referred to in Article 4 of this Agreement, the Governments undertake to provide this contribution in equal amounts. Similarly, any payments made by the Railways to the Governments in terms of section 27 of the Rhodesia Railways Act 1949 of Southern Rhodesia and section 21 of the Rhodesia Railways Ordinance 1949 of Northern Rhodesia, both as amended by the Regulations referred to in Article 4 of this Agreement, will be made to the Governments in equal amounts.

17. Noting the provisions of section 5 of the Rhodesia Railways Act 1949 of Southern Rhodesia and of section 4 of the Rhodesia Railways Ordinance 1949 of Northern Rhodesia, in each case as amended by the Regulations referred to in Article 4 of this Agreement, they recognize the importance in the administration of the undertakings by the Railways on business principles of the application of a commercially sound rating structure, of the maintenance of an efficient and effectively used labour force and of the suitability of the Railways' capital structure and other financial arrangements. In the latter connexion they agree that they will as soon as practicable review in the Higher Authority in consultation with the Railways whether any,

and if so, what changes should be made in the capital structure of the Railways and in the statutory requirements for charges against the revenues of the Railways other than payments in respect of operating and administrative expenses and that they will, so far as may be possible having regard to the financial resources and requirements of the Governments as well as of the Railways, use their best endeavours to effect all necessary changes.

18. They will, as soon as practicable and thereafter from time to time, consider in the Higher Authority, in consultation with the Railways, what level of surplus the latter should endeavour to produce on their net revenue account. This will be determined in the Higher Authority having regard, *inter alia,* to the state of the general reserves of the Railways, to the question of contributions from revenue surpluses to the capital cost of the approved development plan of the Railways and, should the case arise, to the reimbursement to the Governments of any payments that may have been made by them in respect of deficits incurred by the Railways in previous years.

19. They note that the Railways have based their rating structure on the principles recommended in the "Report of the Commission of Inquiry into the Rating Structure of the Rhodesia Railways" dated the 31st March 1959. Any questions which the Governments may wish to raise in connexion with the application or amendment of those principles will be considered in the Higher Authority.

20. They will facilitate transfers of funds by the Railways for the purpose of servicing loans and making other necessary payments in connexion with the Railways' obligations or operations.

21. Except as is provided in existing legislation as amended by the Regulations referred to in Article 4 of this Agreement, the Railways will be exempt from the provisions of any legislation of Southern Rhodesia or of Northern Rhodesia regarding the audit and control of public accounts, and in particular exempt from provisions in such legislation regarding—

(a) the payment of surplus moneys to the Consolidated Revenue Funds or equivalent funds of either Territory;

(b) the submission of capital budgets;

(c) the submission of income and expenditure budgets;

(d) the submission of annual reports and accounts;

(e) the powers of the Comptroller and Auditor General or the official carrying out similar duties in each Territory.

22. They undertake to exempt the Railways from the payment in either Territory of taxes on capital, income or profits.

23. They undertake that they will not impose taxes, fees or other charges on goods or passengers in transit through their Territories by rail in respect of such transit.

Customs

24. Customs and excise duties paid by the Railways or by importers on goods imported and subsequently purchased by the Railways (excluding duties paid on goods for consumption by the general public or by the Railways' staff as private individuals), will so far as practicable be recorded and shared equally between the two Governments.

25. They will adopt in their own customs tariffs the wording and rates of duty appearing against item 138 of the Federal Customs Tariff in force as at the date of dissolution of the Federation and neither Government will vary such wording and rates of duty except after prior consultation with the other.

26. For the purpose of customs and excise duties locomotives, rolling stock, train equipment and spare parts and accessories therefor shall be deemed in the case of new acquisitions by the Railways, to be imported in equal proportions by value simultaneously into the two Territories, and, unless other arrangements are made between the two Governments in respect of local purchases of such items by the Railways, such local purchases shall similarly be deemed to have been made in equal proportions by value simultaneously in both Territories.

27. Locomotives, rolling stock, train equipment and spare parts and accessories therefor, while in the ownership of the Railways, shall be permitted to move freely between the Territories without payment of customs duties.

28. When goods owned by the Railways, other than those mentioned in Article 27 of this Agreement, are removed from one Territory to the other—

(i) if the rate of duty applicable to such goods is the same in both Territories, no duty shall be collected or refunded respectively in the importing and exporting Territories;

(ii) in other cases, whether the goods are new or used,

a refund shall be made of any duty paid in the exporting Territory and any duty payable shall be collected in the importing Territory. For the purpose of both the refund and the collection of duty, the value for duty purposes shall be—

(a) in the case of imported goods, the original import value;

(b) in the case of goods grown, manufactured or produced in either of the Territories, the original value;

less an appropriate allowance in the case of used goods.

29. The detailed application of special Customs arrangements in respect of goods owned by the Railways shall be the subject of agreement between the two Governments, in consultation with the Railways.

Labour

30. They will facilitate the free movement of the Railways' employees between their Territories for railway operating purposes and make special joint arrangements in respect of an[y] liability to customs duties on the used effects of such employees.

31. As this Agreement provides for the continuation of the present body corporate known as the Rhodesia Railways, contracts of employment which exist on 31st December 1963 between the Railways and their employees will continue in force after that date. The Governments accordingly agree that the Railways shall ensure the uninterrupted discharge of their obligations to pensioners and to staff in their employment on that date.

32. They agree on the necessity for the continuation of arrangements for labour relations, including trade union registration, and for the settlement of labour problems by collective bargaining, under special parallel legislation in each Territory applicable to the whole system of the Railways. For this purpose they agree that the Second Schedule to the Rhodesia Railways Act 1949 of Southern Rhodesia and the Schedule to the Rhodesia Railways Ordinance 1949 of Northern Rhodesia will be amended by the Regulations referred to in Article 4 of this Agreement. They also undertake to consider together as soon as possible after the dissolution of the Federation, in consultation with the Railways and their employees, a revision of this legislation to accord with the principles set out in Appendix VI to this Agreement. They contemplate that that revision shall remove differential procedures in the existing legislation by no longer restricting the representation of

African employees to one trade union and by altering the existing arrangements under which the Railway African Workers' Union is not a member of the National Industrial Council.

Traffic Development

33. They recognize that the Railways have been developed to serve the joint needs of the two Territories. They also recognize their mutual interest in the maintenance of the existing arrangements for the movement of their internal and external trade over the Railways as a means of ensuring the viability of the Railways and the protection of their investment in the Railways.

34. They accept the obligations arising from agreements on railway traffic matters which the Government of the United Kingdom has made on their behalf or in respect of each Territory and recognize agreements to which the Railways are a party.

35. In view of the need to place the Railways in a position to relate railway development programmes to probable transport demands, they undertake to provide the Railways annually with their prediction of the general transport needs of each Territory covering a four year period on a year to year basis and to inform the Railways of any potental developments in each Territory which may come to their attention, the implementation of which could result in new or increased traffics suitable for carriage by rail.

36. Whenever either of the Governments views favourably a proposal for the construction of a new railway line, that Government shall inform the Higher Authority and refer the proposal to the Board for an economic and technical appraisal and for the Board's recommendation. The Board shall submit its report on the proposal to the Government concerned which, before pursuing the proposal, shall place it before the Higher Authority for its consideration and approval, together with the Board's report.

37. Any proposal placed before the Higher Authority in accordance with Article 36 of this Agreement shall be considered by the Higher Authority having regard to the provisions of Articles 33 and 34 of this Agreement. The Governments declare that it will be their intention to reach agreement in the Higher Authority on the action to be taken in respect of the proposal. They contemplate that agreement to approve a proposal that would result in financial disadvantage to the Railways may, in appropriate

cases, include provision for an agreed contribution or payment to the Railways by the Government sponsoring the proposal.

38. If a proposal placed before the Higher Authority in accordance with Article 36 of this Agreement relates to a new line not connected to another railway system, nor connecting two lines of the existing system, nor capable of causing a diversion of traffic from the existing system, and the Higher Authority, after considering the report of the Board, does not approve its construction and operation for the account of the Railways, or is unable to agree on the contribution or payment to the Railways mentioned in Article 37 of this Agreement, the Higher Authority may nevertheless direct the Railways to construct and operate the line provided that the Government desiring its construction undertakes:

(i) to provide at a reasonable rate of interest the capital required for the construction and equipment of the line; and

(ii) to pay annually to the Railways a sum equal to the amount, assessed and certified by the Board, by which the revenue derived from the line falls short of the cost of operating and maintaining the line and servicing the capital invested in it and its equipment. This liability shall cease permanently as soon as in any one financial year no payment is due and the Higher Authority is reasonably satisfied that such a state of affairs is likely to continue.

39. If a proposal placed before the Higher Authority in accordance with Article 36 of this Agreement relates to a new line other than a line of the type referred to in Article 38 of this Agreement and the Higher Authority, after considering the report of the Board, does not approve its construction and operation for the account of the Railways or is unable to agree on the contribution or payment to the Railways mentioned in Article 37 of this Agreement, the Higher Authority may nevertheless direct the Railways to construct and operate the line, provided that the Government desiring its construction undertakes:

(i) to provide at a reasonable rate of interest the capital required for the construction and equipment of the line; and

(ii) to pay annually to the Railways a sum equal to the amount assessed and certified by the Board by which the revenue derived from the line falls short of the cost of operating and maintaining the line and of servicing the capital invested in it and its equipment; and

(iii) to pay annually to the Railways a sum equal to the amount assessed and certified by the Board by which the balances on working account in respect of the remainder of the system are reduced by the use of the new line. Any profit obtained in respect of the operation of the new line shall be applied in reduction of these annual sums. Provided that the liability under sub-paragraphs (ii) and (iii) above shall cease permanently as soon as in any one financial year no payment is due under either sub-paragraph and the Higher Authority is reasonably satisfied that such a state of affairs is likely to continue.

40. If the Higher Authority does not agree to direct the Railways to construct and operate a new railway line when the Government desiring this is prepared to give the undertaking mentioned in Article 38 or 39 of this Agreement, as the case may be, that Government may, having regard to the provisions of Articles 33 and 34 of this Agreement, make alternative arrangements for the construction and operation of the line.

41. Whenever either of the Governments views favourably a proposal, other than a proposal for a new railway line, which contemplates diverting traffic previously handled by the Railways or denying it new traffic, that Government, before pursuing the proposal, shall place it before the Higher Authority for its consideration.

42. When a proposal is placed before it in accordance with Article 41 of this Agreement, the Higher Authority shall obtain a report from the Board whether the traffic concerned is within the capacity of the Railways or any expanded capacity to which they are committed, and whether the traffic can be moved competitively by the Railways and what the effect of the proposal would be on the operation and finances of the Railways. The Higher Authority shall consider the proposal in the light of the Board's report and having regard to the provisions of Articles 33 and 34 of this Agreement. If the Higher Authority is agreed that the proposal involves no substantial loss to the Railways, it shall so inform the Government

sponsoring the proposal. If the Higher Authority is not so agreed, it shall report with its recommendations to the Governments on the proposal and the report of the Board shall be annexed thereto.

43. On the submission to them of a report from the Higher Authority in accordance with the provisions of Article 42 of this Agreement, the Governments shall consult together on the proposal with a view to reaching agreement on the action to be taken in respect of it. They contemplate that agreement to approve a proposal may include provision for an agreed payment, by the Government sponsoring the proposal, to the Railways as compensation for the loss that will result to the Railways from the carrying out of the proposal.

44. If they do not agree on the action to be taken on a proposal placed before them in accordance with Article 42 of this Agreement the Government sponsoring the proposal may reach its own decision, having regard to the provisions of Articles 33 and 34 of this Agreement, and, after having notified the Higher Authority of its intention to do so, proceed with the proposal, but in that case it shall pay compensation to the Railways for loss of traffic. In assessing the compensation the object shall be to place the Railways in no worse a position in respect of balances on working account than they would have occupied if the proposal had not been carried out. Accordingly, the assessment shall take into account the benefits as well as the losses to the Railways from the carrying out of the proposal. In particular, the assessment shall take into account:

(a) the effect of the diversion from the Railways of existing traffic and of growth in that traffic for the handling of which the Railways had equipped themselves or were committed to equip themselves at the time the Higher Authority was notified of the intention to proceed with the proposal;

(b) the effect of the denial to the Railways of new traffic within their capacity as described in paragraph (a) above;

(c) the extent to which traffic may be or has been sustained or generated by the carrying out of the proposal;

(d) the ability of the Railways, if the proposal had not been carried out, to carry, at rates economic to their users and competitive with other forms of transport existing at the time mentioned in paragraph (a) above, any new traffic denied to them by the carrying out of the proposal;

(e) the extent to which any increase in traffic actually carried by the Railways may limit or has limited their capacity to carry the traffic diverted from or denied to them.

In the event of the Governments not being able to agree on the sum so payable in any year the matter shall be referred to arbitration in accordance with Article 47 of this Agreement.

45. They undertake to afford the Railways protection from competitive road transport. That protection shall be no less effective than that offered at the time of the signature of this Agreement or shall be such protection as they may agree from time to time.

Bechuanaland

46. They undertake to enter into an Agreement (the agreed draft of which is annexed as Appendix VII) with the Government of the Bechuanaland Protectorate providing for the continuation of the operation and ownership of the railway line in Bechuanaland.

Arbitration

47. They agree that:

(a) in the event of the Higher Authority being unable to render a decision or finding as to any question or matter necessary to the exercise of its functions, or as to any question or matter arising on this Agreement, it may submit the question or matter at issue to an arbitrator or board of arbitration to be appointed by it;

(b) the Higher Authority shall be obliged to submit any such question or matter to an arbitrator or board of arbitration to be appointed by it if the Chairman of the Railways formally requests it to do so on the ground that the question or matter is one of substantial significance for the satisfactory operation of the Railways;

(c) if the Higher Authority is unable to agree on the selection of an arbitrator or board of arbitration, it shall ask the President of the International Bank for Reconstruction and Development, or such other independent authority as the Higher Authority may agree upon, to make a recommendation, which it shall be bound to accept, as to the arbitrator or board of arbitration to be appointed by it;

(d) the Higher Authority shall accept and implement any award made by an arbitrator or board of arbitration appointed in accordance with this Article.

THUS DONE AND SIGNED for and on behalf of the Government of Southern Rhodesia at Salisbury this 10th day of December, 1963.

Witnesses:

1. G. D. Cox   W. J. Harper
2. D. B. Rossiter   Minister of Transport and Power

THUS DONE AND SIGNED for and on behalf of the Government of Northern Rhodesia at Salisbury this 10th day of December, 1963.

Witnesses:

1. N. C. A. Ridley   F. N. Stubbs
2. K. J. Knaggs   Minister of Transport and Works

Index

Index*

Africa (South Central): *maps*, 2, 6, 57; transport regionalism in, 61-63. *See also* Angola; Congo; etc.

Agreements, 4, 9, 14, 53, 59. *See also* Beira Convention; Tripartite Agreement; Zambia-Rhodesia agreement

Agricultural traffic, 14, 17, 21, 31, 41

Anglo-American Corporation, 42, 44

Anglo-Portuguese Convention of 1891, 19

Angola: 36, 53, 59; railways in, 3, 5, 11, 19-20, 22; and recent political changes, 24-27. *See also* Benguela Railways; Lobito; Portugal

BCK (railway): vii, 5, 25-26, 37, 52n; copper freight on, 4, 31; financial position of, 35-36; history of, 15, 22, 23; *map*, 2; and Tripartite Agreement, 14-15, 67-73. *See also* Congo Railways

Bechuanaland, 11, 14n

Beira, Mozambique: 8n; as copper exit, 5, 7, 16, 17, 18, 22, 23, 26, 27, 46-51; rail lines to, 11, 14

Beira Convention: 20, 28, 32; text, 74-81

Belgian Congo. *See* Belgium; Congo

Belgium, 11, 18, 21, 26, 31. *See also* Congo

Benguela Railways: competitive advantages of, 16, 18, 23, 30, 54, 55; copper shipments on, 4, 5, 19, 20, 25-26; financial position of, 35-36; history of, 12-15, 18, 21-23; *map*, 2; proposed investment in, 26, 55, 60; and rate policies, 29-30, 37; and

Tripartite Agreement, 67-73; underutilization of, 20, 23

Benguela-Lobito route. *See* Benguela Railways; Lobito

British South Africa Company (BSA), 12, 13, 19, 22, 23, 44n

Broken Hill, Northern Rhodesia, 11-13

Caminho de Ferro de Benguela (CFB). *See* Benguela Railways

Caminhos de Ferro de Mozambique (CFM). *See* Mozambique Railways

Cape to Cairo railway, 11, 12

Chemin de Fer aux Grands Lacs Africains (CFL). *See* Congo Railways

Chemin de Fer du Bas-Congo au Katanga (BCK). *See* BCK; Congo Railways

Coal, 29, 47, 49-51. *See also* Wankie Colliery

Compensation provision, 29-30

Competition, 18, 30, 36, 37, 39, 40, 53-55, 59, 60

Congo: copper in, 3-4, 7, 8, 9, 20-22, 25, 46-51, 52, 53; and economic integration, 29, 59, 60; hydroelectricity in, 22n; independence of, 4, 9, 17, 18, 24, 26; and past agreements, 32-33; and rate policies, 54-55; and truck transport, 36. *See also* Belgium; National route policy

Congo Railways: 4, 5, 7, 8, 9; history of, 10-11, 13, 15-19, 22-23; *map*, 2. *See also* BCK; Katanga; Matadi; National route policy

Copper: importance of, 1, 3-4; production of, 8, 22; rates on, 36, 39-45, 54; revenues from, 45, 46, 48, 50, 51, 52-53; routes for, 2, 4-9, 13-21,